# Yeshua:
# A Model for
# Moderns

*Leonard Swidler*

**Sheed & Ward**

NOTE: This reprint edition of *Yeshua: A Model for Moderns* contains the additional materials: pp. 49-53, "4. Development and Reinterpretation in the Bible," and pp. 68-69, "4. Yeshua as Jew."

Sheed & Ward™ is a service of The National Catholic Reporter Publishing Company.

Library of Congress Catalog Card Number: 88-61573

ISBN: 1-55612-182-2

Published by:   Sheed & Ward
                115 E. Armour Blvd. P.O. Box 419492
                Kansas City, MO 64141-6492

To order, call: (800) 333-7373

# Contents

# Introduction

In these pages I speak as a modern Christian theologian—not so much about Christ, but about the historical Jesus, or rather, Yeshua, that religious Jew who walked the same earth as I do, almost two thousand years ago. He is not a dead figure to me. He is of the greatest interest not only to me, but also to many moderns. I want to argue that it is Yeshua who is the measure for Christians of what it means to be Christian, who is the model of how to live a full human life. Hence, all doctrines about him must be seen as means to attain a clearer, fuller picture of his historical reality, and not allowed to act as distracting distortions of the focal figure of the Christian religion.

At the same time, the Christian doctrines about the divinity of Christ are not to be waived aside as meaningless. They are in fact attempts to articulate in particular cultural thought categories the encounter with the "transcendent," that which "goes beyond" the every-day, which Christians find in Yeshua. They need to be correctly understood and reexpressed in contemporary thought categories.

Further, when we look at the historical Yeshua through the refracting lenses of the gospels and a few other helpful documents it becomes immediately apparent that he was a Jew, a very devout practicing Jew, until his last breath when he died with a Jewish prayer to the Jewish God on his lips. It also becomes clear that he was not the Messiah expected by the Jews; but he did become the Christ through whom the Gentiles came to know the one true God of the Jews. The fact that Yeshua and his followers were Jewish meant that they also thought and spoke Jewishly, which has profound implications for all subsequent understanding of the Yeshua event.

Although Yeshua provides a model for all on how to live a full human life, he obviously also felt especially responsible for the oppressed of society, and very especially for the largest oppressed class of his and every other society: women. In brief: Yeshua was a feminist. He likewise broke through the stereotypes of the so-called feminine and masculine characteristics and fused them in his own character, thereby providing an androgynous model for all. There is, of course, a whole list of different dimensions of the modelling of a full human life by Yeshua, but the chapter presenting these dimensions is the opening of that project, which the reader can continue on her or his own endlessly.

The final set of reflections here attempts to set a curb on the overweening Christian triumphalism which has traditionally made exclusivistic claims to a life of wholeness, holiness, salvation being possible only along the path of Yeshua the Christ. Not so. The Christian missionary—and all Christians are to be missionaries, that is, ones sent into the world to bear witness to what they have found in Yeshua—in the new dialogic age must not only witness, but also be witnessed to. In a word, s/he must be in dialogue to gain an ever fuller grasp of reality, and the Source of all.

CHAPTER 1

# Yeshua Is the Measure of What It Means to Be Christian

I want to argue that Jesus, Yeshua, is the measure of what it means to be Christian. It might appear at first that this is a very obvious claim that is clearly accepted by all Christians. It may indeed be accepted by all Christians in theory, but I am afraid that it is not accepted by all Christians in the reality of their beliefs. Partly that is because many Christians have a very unclear idea about the meaning and implications of the three main words in that sentence: Jesus, Christian, measure. So let us first clarify the meaning of the words.

## 1. Meaning of Jesus-Yeshua

The name "Jesus," we know, is simply a Latin form of the Greek "Iesous." Actually *Iesous* is not originally a Greek name, but rather a Greek form of a Hebrew name, "Yehoshua" (the biblical "Yoshua") which means "YHWH (probably pronounced *Yahweh*) is salvation." It is not difficult to see how the movement from *Yehoshua*, which in colloquial parlance would sometimes be abbreviated as *Yeshua* or even *Yeshu*, was transliterated into the Greek *Iesous* and the Latin *Jesus*. Unfortunately, in the movement of the name *Yeshua* from its original forms into the various languages used by Christians, and others, something important has been lost. First of all, Jews no longer use the name *Yeshua*, nor indeed do Christians (in fact, both the Hebrew and Greek forms as proper names disappear from usage after the first century).[1] As a result, both Christians and Jews automatically think of Jesus as the name of someone other than a Jew. This simple fact tends to cut Christians off from the taproot of their religion, the Hebrew-Jewish tradition. On the other side it also tends to cut Jews off from a very important son of their tradition, one who has become the most influential Jew of all history, surpassing in historical impact even such giants as Moses, David, Marx, Freud, and Einstein.

1

The name of *Yeshua* is made up of two parts. The first part, "Ye," is an abbreviated form of the Hebrew proper name for God, "YHWH." The second part, "shua," is the Hebrew word for salvation.[2] The word salvation, however, is one that to a large extent has been significantly altered in the Christian tradition from its meaning in Israelite religion and its root meaning in Greek and Latin. It has for the most part been given a restricted meaning since the third century C.E., namely, that when believers in Jesus Christ die, if they have remained faithful, they will go to heaven. But that is not at all what the word basically means. In its Latin form, "salvatio," it comes from the root "salus," [the Greek form is "soterion/soteria" from "saos"] meaning wholeness, health or well-being—hence, "salutary" and "salubrious" in English. The same is true of the Germanic root of the word, "heil," which adjectively also means whole, hale, healed, healthy. Indeed, this is also where the English word "holy" comes from. To be holy means to be whole, to lead a whole, a full life. When we lead a whole, full life, we are holy, we attain salvation, wholeness.[3]

The name Yeshua, then, means YHWH is salvation, wholeness; and the name YHWH is the Hebrew proper name of the one and only God who created everything that exists. We are so used to the concept of monotheism today that we do not realize what an extraordinary breakthrough this insight was in the history of humankind. It had massive immediate implications for how one related to all other human beings and all reality.

If I lived in a nation which had its own god or gods, and all other nations also had their own god or gods, then the ethical rules that were developed by my god's religion would not necessarily be applicable to those persons and things under other gods. Hence, there was not one ethics which was valid for all human beings and for all the earth—until the insight developed that there was in fact one creator God of all human beings and of all reality. So, then, the very name Yeshua is an assertion that YHWH is the source of wholeness for all human beings, for all things. It is a name which carries the very heart of the great contribution of the Hebrew people to humanity, ethical monotheism. Of course there were many Jewish men who were named Yeshua besides Yeshua of Nazareth. However, there is a special appropriateness in the fact that Yeshua of Nazareth was given this name, for it is through him that billions of non-Jews came to the Jewish insight of ethical monotheism, came to YHWH, came to salvation, wholeness.

## 2. Meaning of Christ

It is really quite unfortunate that we Christians have the name that we do. For the term "Christ" is simply a Europeanized version of a Greek translation of a Hebrew title. It was given to a number of Jews during that apocalyptic period shortly before, during and after the lifetime of Yeshua, including Yeshua of Nazareth. It is one of many titles that were given to Yeshua by his followers, one which he almost certainly never used of himself,[4] but rather one which was attributed to him, possibly during his lifetime, by some of his followers. However, there is a special irony in this attribution's having received such prominence, for he was later clearly recognized by his disciples not to be the sort of Messiah that was expected by his enthusiastic Jewish partisans. The Messiah, the Christ, expected by Peter and the other disciples was first thought to be a Jewish royal figure in David's mold who would eject the Roman occupiers of land of Israel and reestablish kingship in Israel. Clearly this did not happen; hence most Jews had no grounds for assuming that Yeshua was the promised Messiah.

Probably not all of his followers were set on seeing him as the promised Messiah but viewed him in other ways, for example, as a prophet or teacher (rabbi). But those who did think of him as the promised Messiah were ready to admit after his crucifixion that they were mistaken. This is clearly reflected, for example, in Luke's Gospel where two of Yeshua's followers on the way to Emmaus spoke of him as "a prophet" and, after referring to his crucifixion, added in disappointment, "but our own hope had been that he would be the one to set Israel free." (Luke 24:21)

After the resurrection experience, however, some of Yeshua's followers apparently slowly began to decide not to abandon the term Messiah but to transform it, to read it in a different sense. Eventually the term Messiah or Christ became something like the preferred title for him, often functioning as a kind of surname. However, all this took some time and it was not until later in the first century that the followers of Yeshua were referred to as "Christians." As the Acts of the Apostles tells it, the term first used was followers of "The Way," that is, the way to lead a whole, holy life, a Jewish life, which had been taught and exemplified by Yeshua of Nazareth.

It would of course make most sense if the followers of Yeshua had given themselves a name related to his name Yeshua. However, the only term widely used among Christians which in fact relates to the name of Yeshua, or rather Jesus, unfortunately has picked up a very negative connotation and stands for precisely the opposite of what Yeshua himself stood for: Jesuitical.

3

## 3. Meaning of Measure

Nevertheless, I still wish to make the claim that Jesus, Yeshua, is the standard, the measure by which everything is to be judged in answering the question whether or not it is Christian. But to do this it is also important that we be clear about what we mean when we say that something is the measure or standard of something else. We are talking about mainly a set of beliefs, or doctrines, including rules for conduct, which we refer to in short-hand fashion with the terms "faith and morals." For the sake of simplicity and clarity let us refer to the teachings in these two areas as doctrines, which of course means precisely "that which is taught," coming from the Latin word "docere," to teach.

A teaching or doctrine is a "reaction to" a person or an event. A doctrine is something which arises in bi-polar fashion. There is the initial event and then the person who reacts to it. The initial event of course cannot simply be "repeated." It must somehow be assimilated by the observing person. Otherwise it will remain simply a past fact which has no effect on anyone's life. If an initial event is to develop into a teaching or doctrine a person or persons must somehow perceive it and state its significance. It is that understanding and expression that transmits and determines the direction and form of the power of the initial event in the lives of living persons. A number of persons may perceive the same event with some reacting with total indifference and others reacting positively or negatively in a great variety of ways. Precisely that "reaction to," that understanding and expression of the significance of the initial event, is the power-transmitting and shaping instrument which we call doctrine or teaching.

Hence, when we speak of the doctrine of what it means to be Christian, or Christology, it is not sufficient to attempt to point to or "repeat" the Yeshua-event. In fact, it is impossible to do so. Living persons must somehow perceive the Yeshua-event and respond to it with something more than indifference to produce a doctrine which will have an effect on their lives.

In the history of Christianity many persons have in various ways perceived the Yeshua-event and have reacted to it vigorously. It has often produced a deep effect on their lives. But not all actual "reactions to" the Yeshua-event, that is, not all doctrines of Christology, have been or are now accepted by all committed Christians. No concerned Christian can affirm, for example, both the world-fleeing Christologies of some Gnostic Christians (which in fact were traditionally rejected as heterodox) and the world-affirming Christologies of the synoptic gospels. Somewhere Christians must have a measuring stick by which to judge a "correct" Christology. For some, it is contemporary Church authority (*magisterium*). For others, it is past Church authority (*traditio*), either in whole or in part (e.g., the first seven Ecumenical Councils). For still others it is the authority of the Scriptures (*sola Scriptura*), although many Protestants now recognize that Scripture itself is simply the earliest set of traditions.

Today historically-minded Christian thinkers are putting forth a christological method that attempts to go behind the authority of tradition (whether *magisterium, traditio, or Scriptura*) and locate the initial event fundamentally not in any foreshortened "reaction to," or doctrine about, the Yeshua-event, but in the Yeshua of history himself. Living Christians must as best as possible apprehend and "react to" this Yeshua of history, that is, the Yeshua of Nazareth who lived in Israel two thousand years ago. It is no longer sufficient in a world that is historically conscious for Christians to "react to" earlier "reactions to," doctrines about, the Yeshua-event. Historically-conscious persons want to base their judgments and actions as much as possible on the primary facts, and for Christians the primary facts are preeminently that Jew, the historical person Yeshua of Nazareth, standing as he did fully in the Hebraic and Judaic traditions as they had developed up to his time and then were given the particular interpretation he set forth.

## 4. The Yeshua of History

With the help especially of the historical-critical method, but also of other critical scholarly methods, such as literary criticism, we are now able to perceive the major outlines of the actual teachings of Yeshua who had such a massive impact on his followers. This perception, of course, will continue to be refined, but the essential elements are reasonably sure. We must bear in mind that it was only in the beginning of the nineteenth century that a sense of history as we now understand it developed in any civilization. One consequence was that Christian thinkers and scholars began the search for the "historical Jesus," the Yeshua of Nazareth who lay behind the many conflicting things said about him in the past two thousand years. Up until that time his teachings, contained in the gospels, were known as those of all the figures of antiquity are known, namely, as transmitted by his disciples.

Early in this century with the development of certain critical tools it was perceived that the sources of our image of the historical Yeshua, the gospels, were not primarily historical documents—four different modern biographies—but rather four separate faith statements based on historical reminiscences. The gospels communicated what various early followers of Yeshua understood and believed to be of the greatest importance about him, his teachings and actions, and his final "exaltation in glory." For several decades beginning about 1918—although the tendency went back to S. H. Reimarus (d. 1768)—there was great scepticism among New Testament scholars concerning the possibility of getting behind the "Christ of faith" to the "Yeshua of history." That astringent phase is now largely over so that it is possible to state with confidence: "It is today a broadly held consensus that, although because of the nature of the sources it is impossible to produce a biography of Jesus, the description of the irreplaceable fundamental characteristics of his proclamation, his action and his fate, on the other hand, is very much possible."[5] This is the statement of a Catholic systematic theologian, Hans Küng, who here quite accurately reflects the view and work of a growing number of New Testament exegetical scholars, Catholic, Protestant and Jewish. One of them, E. P. Sanders, refers to the works of ten of his most prestigious colleagues, including Martin Hengel, Paul Winter, Joachim Jeremias, Edouard Schweizer, C. H. Dodd, and Geza Vermes, writing that "the dominant view today seems to be that we can know pretty well what Jesus was out to accomplish, that we can know a lot about what he said, and that those two things make sense in the world of first-century Judaism."[6] The Jewish scholar Geza Vermes argues that, "we can manage to perceive his ideas, the *ipsissimus sensus,* even without the actual words in which they were formulated."[7]

It is that Yeshua of history, then, the one who lived in the land of Israel two thousand years ago, who can clarify for contemporary Christians what must be the touchstone for all "reactions to," that is, all "doctrines" about, him, including the various ones in the New Testament itself.[8] It may not be objected that the image of the historical Yeshua produced by the help of the historical method is simply a contemporary "image" and can make no more claim to allegiance by Christians than any other "image" of Yeshua, as, for example, that of Paul, who never knew Yeshua, or a Gnostic Christian, or the Council of Chalcedon (451 C.E.). In fact, there is nothing in any living person's mind that is not an "image." But there is a fundamental difference between the image formed of a person from the words and actions of the person him or herself and the image formed from what someone else thinks of that person.

I am aware of the grave difficulties of arriving at an authoritative, clear image of the historical Yeshua. But to the extent that we Christians can, we must. That must be our standard. Of course no one can ever arrive at a completely "objective" image of Yeshua. Every fact is relativized by the perceiver. It is also true that we can come to a fuller grasp of a fact if we have perceptions of it from several different standpoints. It is, however, the original datum, the *Urtatsache,* that we are trying to grasp so that we can somehow relate it to ourselves. This latter part of course again relativizes the original fact, i.e., puts it in relation to us, but it is the *Urtatsache* that we are trying to grasp and relate to us. We know today that we can never fully grasp it as it "objectively" originally existed—just as in modern physics we now realize that to pass light or electrons or whatever through an object so as to "observe" it already changes it. Still, with that now chastened knowledge that we can never attain a completely "objective" image of anything, we can always strive to come closer, as with the Parmenidian continuum. It is this that I and a growing number of Christian thinkers believe we should do in regard to the historical figure of Yeshua.

Then, with due modesty and openness, it seems to me that the best image of the historical Yeshua that we are able to attain at a given moment has priority over all explanations as to his meaning. *What Yeshua thought, taught and wrought is the Yeshuanic, if not the "Christian," Gospel,* even though we learn that only through others. Edward Schillebeeckx makes the same claim: "The constant factor in Christianity is that Christians determine the final or ultimate meaning of their concrete history by reference to Jesus of Nazareth."[9] Things are said to be Christian "with the same proviso that they are judged to conform to the yardstick of this historical reality that is Jesus himself."[10]

Each person stands in a particular historical context and place in the world so that all perceptions are fundamentally influenced by that fact, including perceptions of historical-critical images. An awareness of this limitation will allow a person to avoid naive absolute certitude on the one hand and total scepticism on the other. Further, as we become aware that human language is both a liberating and a limiting instrument, we will be able to proceed with modesty though also security, always being open to new evidence, insights, perspectives, and, hence, change. But of course all this proper modesty is appropriate not only for the image of the historical Yeshua that is derived from the "primary data," but also, and all the more so, for all images of the "reactions to," or doctrines about, him.

What does a contemporary Christian do, however, with the historical fact that in the development of Christianity the "teaching Yeshua" quickly became the "taught Christ," even within the time of the writing of the New Testament? Clearly the resurrection experience was a transforming one for the followers of Yeshua. However one understands the New Testament reports of the empty tomb, the resurrection experience had a profound impact on the followers of Yeshua: They began to perceive things about him that they had not been conscious of when they were with him. Clearly, however, the Yeshua they knew was not transformed into some kind of magic figure or totem for them. Rather, in the resurrection experience the followers of Yeshua felt first of all inwardly confirmed in their pre-crucifixion experience of the encounter with what they perceived to be the divine through Yeshua, through what he thought, taught and wrought.

## 5. The Teaching Yeshua, Not the Taught Christ

The New Testament scholar Thomas William Mansion remarked: "We are so accustomed, and rightly, to make Jesus the object of religion that we become apt to forget that in our earliest records he is portrayed not as the object of religion, but as a religious man."[11]

Thus, in teaching (about) Yeshua his followers attempted to teach what they had learned from him. However, what they learned from Yeshua could not be limited to what he put into words (what Yeshua "taught"); they obviously were deeply struck by his inner self, which appeared to them to be so full of wisdom and effective love (what Yeshua "thought"), and how this seemed to them to exude into his every action (what Yeshua "wrought"). This is evident in the synoptic reportage. Yeshua's whole person was the source of this utterly transforming "learning experience" for his followers. This transformation was so profound, so pervasive, that, rather than being shattered by the shattering of Yeshua on the cross (its agony proved to be the crucible in which their "enlightenment" and love were purified, strengthened, transformed), they were enabled, as it were, in Pauline symbolic language, to go down into the tomb with him and rise with the reconfirmation of their pre-crucifixion experience of Yeshua, that is: their experience of him was true, authentic, after all; he really was— is!—the source of true life; he lives on! Thus the "taught Yeshua" (i.e., the taught or proclaimed Christ) was first of all the fullest way to hand on the "teaching Yeshua," that is, what he thought, taught and wrought in his *whole* person. Hence, it appears to many Christian thinkers that any move to understand the proclaimed Christ as someone, something, other than the "teaching Yeshua" can easily become problematic. Any move to understand the "proclaimed Christ" in contrast to the "teaching Yeshua," to what he "thought, taught and wrought" in his whole person, would be to play false not only with Yeshua but also his first disciples.

The theology of the Gospel of Luke is even clearer in its insistence that it is primarily what Yeshua preached, rather than Yeshua himself, that should be preached by Christians. The Catholic Scripture scholar Joseph G. Kelly notes that, according to Luke, "Jesus always points not to himself but to God. As a result, the preacher cannot become the preached.... The disciples are not called upon to preach the person of Jesus. What they must do is preach the message of Jesus.... Jesus shows Christians the Way and Christians see themselves on the Way." Therefore, Kelly says, what Christians must now preach is the Way which Yeshua preached; that is: repentance and the forgiveness of sins—release (Lk. 4:18). This Way is to be preached in the name of Yeshua and followed by Yeshua's disciples because he was the one who accomplished this Way. But, for Luke, "Jesus is not the Way. The Way is what Jesus taught must be done. The message is not Jesus, but release. Jesus did not glorify himself, but lived in such a way as to give glory to God. This resulted in God's glorifying Jesus. Jesus did not proclaim himself but said that his person and life made God known." Kelly adds that "every time that the reign breaks in at a moment of release, one can glimpse God. God is the end and the goal. One of the ways to find God is to follow the Way of Jesus, but Jesus' Way is not the only way."[12]

Imbedded in the Gospels of Matthew and Luke is a prior document which New Testament scholars refer to as "The Sayings of Jesus," or "Q" (from the German word *Quell,* source). Analyists of Q, which is "one of the earliest writings, if not the earliest writing in Christianity,"[13] find in these reflections of perhaps the first Christians an understanding of Yeshua "almost entirely different from what we find in Paul, and its [Q] view of Christianity challenges us to rethink the very beginnings of Christianity itself."[14]

These scholars also note that in Q Yeshua the proclaimer does not become the proclaimed, "but in Q he remains the proclaimer," and that "this is the very heart of Q's understanding of the way of salvation. Jesus himself is the very means of salvation, but it is not through his redeeming death, which is nowhere mentioned in Q, rather, in his revealing of God's reign and the way to share in that kingdom."[15] In other words, salvation, authentic human life, is to be found by following what Yeshua taught. Moreover, when Yeshua says in Q "whoever rejects me rejects him who sent me" (Lk. 10: 16), "of course, the sending from the Father does not refer to the incarnation of Jesus, but to Jesus' call to be a prophet."[16]

Most Christians over the centuries have from the beginning understood the historical Yeshua, what he thought, taught and wrought, to be centrally important. It has for the most part been argued that a particular teaching about Yeshua was right, orthodox, because it ultimately fit with the historical Yeshua who lived two thousand years ago. True, some teachings were directly based only on some later *traditio,* but then the claim was at least implicit that such a procedure was a sure way to link up with the real, historical Yeshua. There would be few Christians, if any, who would be willing to affirm the statements about Jesus Christ in the Council of Nicaea (325 C.E.) or Constantinople (381 C.E.) *even if* they could not be said of the historical Yeshua of Nazareth. The difficulty that historically conscious scholars point to in this situation is that the "reactions to," the statements about, Yeshua, whether past (*traditio*) or present (*magisterium*), tend too often to be the yardstick for understanding the historical Yeshua, when it should be the other way around.

In a recent book that has a great deal to recommend it in its expansive and balanced view, the Catholic theologian William M. Thompson alludes to the "historical Jesus" and rejects him as "a final norm of Christian revelation and theology." One reason offered for this rejection is that our knowledge of the Jesus of history "must ultimately rely upon the kerygma [proclamation]."[17] The assertion is true, but how does that not make the historical Yeshua the ultimate standard? Of course, for us it is our apprehension of the historical Yeshua, derived from a critical analysis of the kerygmatic text, that *de facto* is our final norm. But that is also true of the kerygmatic Yeshua, the "previously 'reacted to'" Yeshua—only one step still further removed from the historical Yeshua. Mark, Matthew, Paul, Chalcedon, etc., all believed and averred that they were communicating something very important about the historical Yeshua. They did not want their readers to accept it because they said it but because it told them something important about the real, historical Yeshua, which would lead them to live a full human, i.e., "saved" life. For a subsequent Christian to claim that their statements, their *kerygma* of (preaching about, reactions to) the historical Yeshua is the ultimate norm of what is authentically Christian is either to miss or reject the very essence of what they were saying. To be sure, the gospels are the final documentary sources we have for our knowledge of Yeshua. But the point to be noticed here is that they are "documents," i.e., "teachings," and teachings are of or about something and/or someone—in this case, Yeshua. The "documents" are merely the pointers to, images, (*eidola*) of, the historical reality referred to. To stop short finally at the *eidola* rather than move on toward that which *eidola* point to is *(e)ido-latria*.

## 6. Yeshua: Messiah or Christ?

If Yeshua taught that the Torah should be observed (which he did—see chapter 2), should his followers then observe the Torah? Put that way, the answer seems an obvious "Yes." And that is precisely what all his first followers thought too, and they acted accordingly. Peter and the other disciples and followers went to pray at the Temple and synagogue and observed the Torah. But then after awhile as their teaching spread there arose the problem of the gentiles. Could they also become followers of The Way? The first answer was "Yes." The Jews had already been making converts for scores of years. These gentile converts to Judaism were called proselytes; they were circumcised and took on the full observance of the Torah.

But in the synagogues outside of Israel there were not only born Jews and proselytes, but also the so-called "God-fearers," who apparently were much more numerous than the proselytes. The God-fearers were gentiles who accepted the teachings, ethics, Scriptures, and main cultic practices such as the Sabbath, but were not circumcised and did not follow all the ritual laws of Judaism. It was from among them that many of the first followers of The Way outside of Israel came. At first they were often told they had to become full-fledged Jews in order to be followers of The Way (to be Jewish), to be followers of Yeshua. It made sense, but not complete sense to all. The scores of thousands of God-fearers in the Roman empire had earlier decided to throw in their lot with Judaism, but not including circumcision and the full observance of the Torah. Why should they change that decision in order to be associated with one particular Way of being Jewish?

The obvious direct way to solve that problem was to inquire what Yeshua had to say on the matter. Unfortunately he had said nothing. As we read over the gospels it appears that Yeshua felt himself sent "only to the lost sheep of the people of Israel" (Mt. 15:24), as he told his disciples, and that when he sent out the Twelve to preach the Good News he said to them, "Do not go to any gentile territory or any Samaritan towns. Go instead to the lost sheep of the people of Israel" (Mt. 10:5). However, when gentiles came to him he responded to them—he healed the child of the Syro-Phoenecian woman and of the centurion. Thus it would seem that the teachings and actions of Yeshua did not speak directly to his later followers' problem, a situation the like of which is bound to occur frequently in every movement.

Hence the early Jewish followers of Yeshua had to solve their problem by applying the spirit of the teaching and life of Yeshua, what he thought, taught and wrought, to their contemporary situation. They decided, after an intense struggle between Peter and Paul, along the lines of the God-fearers' solution: those who were born Jews had received the privilege and burden of the Torah and should, as Yeshua himself taught and did, continue to observe it; those who were not should simply accept the Jewish teachings, Scriptures, ethics, and main cultic customs as focused through

Yeshua, but they did not have to take on circumcision and the full obligation of the Torah, especially the ritual customs.[18]

But something else very critical happened in this early gestation period of the Christian religion. Yeshua had taught his followers to live a life that was intensely, interiorly, and in prophet-like concern for the oppressed, faithful to God's Torah. His followers also thought after a while that he was the promised "anointed one" of God, the *Meshiach,* the Messiah, who was to overthrow Israel's yoke of Roman occupation and become king. Yeshua told them often that his kingdom was not to be a political one, but they nevertheless set their hearts wildly on the imminent in-breaking of God's reign. (This was not unheard of in the Judaism of that time, as it languished under the foreign oppression of the Roman empire. There were many messianic claimants. For example, a hundred years after the death of Yeshua, Rabbi Akiba, who is highly revered in the Jewish community to this very day, proclaimed that the anti-Roman Jewish Freedom Fighter Bar Kochba—who went down to defeat in 135 C.E.—was the *Meshiach.*) But those high, wild-hearted hopes were crushingly dashed on Good Friday. All seemed destroyed. They said, "This man was a prophet, and was considered by God and by all the people to be mighty in words and deeds. Our chief priests and rulers handed him over to be sentenced to death, and they nailed him to the cross. And we had hoped that he would be the one who would set Israel free" (Lk. 24:19-21).

However, as we know, it did not all end there. Three days after Good Friday was Easter, the Resurrection event. The followers of Yeshua experienced him now not only as the charismatic teacher who was ignominiously executed, but also as the one raised up to a new life by God.

In light of the extraordinary, energizing Easter experience the followers of Yeshua, as noted above, began to reflect on everything he had said and done. They thus began to see things they were unaware of at the time. More and more they were convinced that God had been doing great things in Yeshua. As they reflected they tried to name these great things, and so Yeshua was retrospectively given various titles: Lord, Savior, Son of Humanity, Son of God, etc. One title, *Meshiach,* was still attributed to him, as it perhaps was during his historical life, but now inwardly transformed, "spiritualized." It comes down to us from the New Testament Greek as *Christos,* Christ. Thus it is more accurate to say that Christians claim that Yeshua, crucified and raised up, is not the *Meshiach,* Messiah, as promised in the Scriptures—for among other things a political leader, a king who would liberate the country Israel and bring universal peace was promised—but is the Christ, somehow a meeting point of the human and divine.

Thus in short order Yeshua, the Christ, became the door through which the gentiles enter into the knowledge (not just of the head but also of the heart, and not just individually but also communally) of the one God, the Creator, the Source and Goal of all being, and of how they should live according to God's design, God's Torah. Because many gentiles came to the one true God through Yeshua the Christ, as we saw, they called themselves Christians. But most born Jews in effect said: "Yeshua, yes—Messiah or Christ, no. Yeshua clearly did not fulfill the promises of the *Meshiach,* and we are not in need of a Christ to bring us to the one true God we know God already."

## 7. Yeshua and His Disciples Thought Jewishly

We now come to an extremely crucial and delicate point which follows from the Jewishness of Yeshua and his first followers, the founders of The Way, of Christianity. Because they were all Jews, they thought and talked like Jews. Consequently, if we are to understand correctly what Yeshua and his first followers meant when they spoke, we will have to perceive their statements in their Jewish categories and thought patterns. Not to do so would be to read *our* foreign meaning into their statements and actions rather than to draw out *their* intended meaning. We would be engaged in *eis*egesis instead of *ex*egesis. The Catholic systematic theologian Edward Schillebeeckx stressed this when he wrote "Jesus was a Jew; and his close friends and disciples also thought as faithful Jews would think. It was as Jews that they were to interpret Jesus."[19]

Those Christians who have gone the route of seeking out interpretations of the words and actions of Yeshua and his first followers that are different than Jewish understandings have obviously turned away from Yeshua and the founders of Christianity. To be sure, there were disputes among the Jews themselves about the correct meaning of many things. But these disputes all took place within an accepted framework of meaning. It is within that broad Jewish framework of meaning that Yeshua and the founders of the The Way thought and acted. Consequently, it is also the framework within which subsequent followers of Yeshua will have to understand Yeshua and his followers first if they are to grasp their message, their "good news," correctly. Of course, ways of thinking other than Jewish can be of great value, and Christians certainly are to be encouraged to embrace everything of value. Non-Jewish ways of thinking, however, will not be of value in understanding what Yeshua and his first followers said and did. In fact, they can be extremely misleading and even funda-

mental hindrances to the "Good News," the Gospel of Yeshua and his first
followers if so applied.

Such a principle of understanding appears quite straightforward and
simple. But the grasp of this simple principle depends on perceiving all
statements about the meaning of things to be relational, that is, properly
understood only when seen in relation to the persons who made the statements, the contexts in which they made them, the patterns of thought and
speech they used, etc. Such a perception is standard fare for a contemporary Western scholar—post historicism, sociology of knowledge, and linguistic analysis. Not so, however, in the past. This principle of understanding the Gospel relationally, that is, within the Jewish framework of
meaning that Yeshua and his first followers embraced, simple and obvious
as it seems to many today, will occasion in many instances a radical re-
thinking of Christian teaching, to bring it in line with the thought of
Yeshua and his first followers, the founders of The Way, Christianity—to
bring it in line with their Jewish way of understanding.

Let us illustrate the implications of applying this principle of understanding by looking again, however briefly, at the central teaching of
Christianity, one upon which everything else depends: Christology.

As noted above, it is clear that Yeshua's followers thought of him during his life-time as the *Meshiach,* with all its political implications, etc.,
although, judging from contemporary Scripture scholarship, it is unlikely
that Yeshua himself ever claimed to be the *Meshiach.*[20] But even if he did
think of and claim himself to be the *Meshiach,* it was in very transformed,
"spiritualized" fashion; the same was also true of his followers after the
crucifixion and resurrection event. In any case, Jews never thought of the
*Meshiach* (and who else thought of a *Meshiach* but a Jew?) as being divine
in an ontological sense. The *Meshiach* was called a son of God by Jews,
but again, never in an ontological sense. For the Jews, this language was
always understood in a non-ontological, metaphorical sense. And Yeshua
and his first followers were Jews. They thought and spoke as Jews. Consequently, when speaking of Yeshua as *Meshiach,* or even in the transformed, spiritualized sense of *Christos,* these Jews were not speaking ontologically. It was not the Jews, it should be recalled, but the Greeks who
developed the ontological framework of thinking—*philosophia.* Pouring
ontological meaning into the non-ontological Jewish language of Yeshua
and his first—Jewish—followers again is to engage not in exegesis but in
eisegesis.

But what about the christological dogmas of the Councils of Nicaea,
Constantinople, and Chalcedon? Are they not full of ontological meanings? However they are to be interpreted—e.g., as attempts to articulate

the Christian experience of the transcendent in Yeshua, as will be discussed below—surely they should be understood in the light of what Yeshua and his first followers understood themselves to be teaching—and they understood themselves Jewishly, i.e., non-ontologically in these matters.

Is there not a clear logic in contemporary Christians' taking as a basic standard of the meaning of Yeshua the explanation given by the chief of the Apostles, Peter (presumably his testimony would be especially weighty with his "successor," the pope, and the 800 million Catholics): "Jesus of Nazareth, a man (*andra*) attested to you by God with...signs which God did through him.... God raised him up.... This Jesus God raised up.... God has made him both lord and Christ" (Acts 2:22, 24, 32, 36)? Here it is clear that Peter thought of Yeshua as a man (*andra*) in whom God was manifested through "mighty works and wonders and signs," who was killed and then raised to a new life as "lord and Christ" by God. If the first followers of Yeshua, after the resurrection event (led by no less a figure than Peter, according to Luke), held such a "low" Christology, should such a position not enjoy the greatest of respect? Is such a "low" Christology simply "lifted up," *aufgehoben,* by a "high" Christology which speaks of Yeshua as man and God, or is it in fact "swallowed up" and changed from a Jewish to a Hellenistic way of thinking—without being aware that the Jewish way is basically non-ontological, metaphorical, and thereby misunderstanding it?

## 8. Yeshua, Human and Divine

But what of those christological dogmatic formulas hammered out in the ancient ecumenical councils to which assent was demanded under pain of excommunication? If accepted, do they not wipe out any "low Christology" and require a specific "high Christology," namely, according to Chalcedon (451 C.E.), that Yeshua is "truly a human being and truly God" (*vere homo et vere Deus*)? Obviously an old style catechism-like yes or no answer is not appropriate. One must first get clear about precisely what the Chalcedonian formula meant. To do that it is not sufficient even to come to understand the meanings of the various terms and images used in that intellectual milieu, especially in this instance, for the authors were dealing in part with that which "goes beyond" our experience, the "transcendent." If taken literally, their language was non-sense. It spoke of a non-thing, or no-thing, for the Council Fathers spoke of Yeshua being a "limited unlimited," a "finite infinite." But obviously they did not mean to say no-thing—even deliberately paradoxical language does not intend to communicate literal non-sense, but attempts to point to some reality beyond the apparent non-sense of the contradictory terms juxtaposed. The reader here then has the first task of discerning what meaning the authors were pointing to beyond and by way of the seeming non-sense of the juxtaposed mutually exclusive terms *homo* and *Deus*.[21]

To begin with, there is no reason to assume that the way the ancient Christian authors expressed the meaning they were attempting to communicate was necessarily the best possible, the clearest, the most helpful, etc. The very fact that the ancient Christians had to go back into council time and again over the same basic question (Nicaea, 325; Constantinople, 381; Ephesus, 431; Chalcedon, 451) amply demonstrates this point. I believe these ancient Christians were trying to express in Greek philosophical, ontological terms the Christian experience of the overwhelming confluence of the human and divine in *Yeshua ha Notzri*.

However, the ontological question was not one that excited the Semitic world. Jews tended to ask axiological rather than ontological questions: not questions of being, but of doing ("What must I *do* to gain eternal life?" not "What must I *be* or *think* to gain eternal life" was asked of Yeshua—the Jew). This is seen reflected in the entire history and structure of Judaism; it is not the creed or doctrine that holds pride of place but the *halahkah*, the rules of ethics or just action.[22]

If it is granted that the Christians meeting at Chalcedon might not have communicated their meaning in the most helpful, clearest possible language, I would then want to move from that subjunctive to the indicative mood. I am persuaded they did not express themselves as clearly, helpfully as possible for all ages to come. I would suggest that their meaning would be better expressed by using adjective rather than noun forms, that is, instead of saying Yeshua is "truly a human being and truly God," *vere homo et vere Deus*, it would be clearer to say that Yeshua is "truly human and truly divine," *vere humanus et vere divinus*. The paradoxical quality of the first statement is retained in the second in that the two terms, human and divine, appear to go in opposite directions, but the juxtaposition of the two does not result in non-sense: it is conceiv*able* that someone could in some way be truly human and truly divine. In what way not only *might* this be, but in what way *was* this affirmed to be true of Yeshua?

There is no question but that not only in the earliest layers of the Christian "good news" Yeshua is portrayed as and understood to be truly human, but also even the "highest" orthodox Christian christological formulas (like that of Chalcedon) insisted on that. But, the followers of Yeshua, especially upon post-resurrection-event reflection, perceived God working in and through him in an extraordinary manner.[23] To them, God appeared to be manifesting her/himself through him. It seemed to them that Yeshua was so completely open to all dimensions of reality, of being (as all human beings, as intellectual cognitive beings, also are *in principle*), that he was totally suffused with an inpouring of being in a "radical," that is, in a "to the roots" way, which included the "Root," the Source of all being—in theistic language, God. Thus one could meaningfully say that Yeshua was fully, truly divine. That is, because he was fully open to all being and the Source of being there was no part of him that was not permeated with the Source of being.

It would seem that at this point many Hellenistic Christians of the patristic age made the linguistic move of saying that because Yeshua was permeated with the Source of being, with God, he therefore could also meaningfully be said to *be* truly God. But linguistically that was a confusing rather than a clarifying move because such language inadvertently also suggests that God is co-terminous with Yeshua.

That is: God is infinite, unlimited, whereas human beings, as well as all other beings, are finite, limited. However, to say that Yeshua *is* God is to say that Yeshua, a human being and therefore finite, *is* not finite, but infinite. Or, in other words: to form a sentence linking together with the nexus *is* the subject and predicate when both are nouns and at least one is exhaustive of its category can only mean that the subject and predicate are co-terminous. For example, if there is only one President of the United States, the statement that "Reagan is president" means that there is no specific Reagan that is not president and no president that is not Reagan; Reagan and president are limited to each other. Or: "Yeshua is God" means that there is no specific Yeshua that is not God and no God that is not Yeshua; Yeshua and God are limited to each other.

But that of course was not what was intended, for Christians did not wish to imply that the unlimited God was limited to Yeshua. Hence, to avoid this unintended non-sense, it would help to use the adjective form "divine" rather than the noun form "God," since the former term does not limit the Unlimited to the limited, which the latter term does.

Edward Schillebeeckx makes a similar point when he writes that:

> since 1953 I have firmly opposed the formulation "Christ is God and man" and also the confusing expression "the man Jesus is God." The proper formula would be: "Jesus Christ is the Son of God *in humanity*." The deepest sense of revelation is that God reveals himself in humanity. We cannot seek farther, above or beneath the man Jesus his being-God. The divinity must be perceptible *in* his humanity itself.[24]

To repeat: to say that "Yeshua is God," if both the subject and the predicate, Yeshua and God, are understood as nouns, clearly means that Yeshua and God are coextensive, that is, there is no Yeshua that is not God and there is no God that is not Yeshua. But that is obviously *not* what Christians, whether early or current, mean to claim. Hence, it would appear unavoidable to conclude that in this sentence although Yeshua is meant as a noun, God is not meant as a noun but as an adjective. To make that clearly implied but confusedly disguised meaning explicitly clear, it would therefore be helpful to make the predicate specifically adjectival in form: "Yeshua is divine." Such a sentence is not non-sense and appears to capture precisely what Christians mean to say with the confusing sentence, "Yeshua is God."

But what of those passages in the New Testament itself which seem to state clearly that Yeshua is God and have been traditionally so understood, i.e., Paul's Epistle to the Philippians 2:5-11, and the Prologue to John's Gospel? Can they just be waved aside as the Hellenizing of the original Jewish understanding of Yeshua?

Of course, if it is *assumed* ahead of time that the concept of Yeshua as the incarnation of the second person of the Blessed Trinity existing from all eternity could have been in the mind of the Pharisaic Jew Paul in the middle of the first century, then the words of the hymn that Paul recites in his letter to the followers of Yeshua at Philippi can be so understood.[25] But Paul wrote three hundred years before the Council at Nicaea and four hundred years before the one at Chalcedon when this concept was hammered out—not by Jews, but by Hellenistic Christians who were triumphant over Jews and everyone else in the Roman empire. As E. P. Sanders has pointed out, "It is true that the early Church came to believe that Jesus was a transcendent being.... But it would be foolhardy—or worse—to rush to the conclusion that the historical Jesus must have corresponded to such beliefs."[26]

## 9. Pre-existent Christ?

In fact, reasonable principles of interpretation would indicate that the words of Paul should be understood in the way he and his readers would have understood them—and Paul too was a Jew, in fact, "a Hebrew of the Hebrews, according to the Law a Pharisee" (Phil. 3:5).

For a very long time Paul was read through non-Jewish lenses, and as a result he was often gravely misunderstood. It is only in very recent times that scholars, Christian and Jewish, have begun to read Paul through Jewish lenses, thereby coming much closer to what Paul actually meant and how he was understood by his first—mostly Jewish—readers. This is clearly the method any serious student of Paul must follow.

Geza Vermes points out that,

> To a Greek speaker in Alexandria, Antioch or Athens at the turn of the eras, the concept *huios theou,* son of God, would have brought to mind either one of the many offspring of the Olympian deities.... But to a Jew, the corresponding Hebrew or Aramaic phrase would have applied to none of these. For him, son of God could refer...to a good Jew; or to a charismatic holy Jew; or to the king of Israel; or.... In other words *"son of God" was always understood metaphorically in Jewish circles.*

He goes on to make the very interesting observation that, "If the medium in which Christian theology developed had been Hebrew and not Greek, it would not have produced an incarnation doctrine as this is traditionally understood."[27]

This position is supported by the Christian exegete James Barr who argues that Paul and other Jews probably understood Paul's hyperbolic references to Yeshua in typically Jewish metaphorical fashion, but that as heard by Hellenistic ears they probably were misconstrued in a non-metaphorical sense:

> It could be argued that this emphasis upon the Hebraic background of ideas may indeed have been present in the minds of instructed Jews like St. Paul, but that the words which had this series of associations for him could for the most part be *understood* by Gentile Christian hearers, especially by the less instructed among them, in the normal Hellenistic sense of the words.[28]

In fact, the Jewish-Christians, the so-called Ebionites, "became convinced that they were witnessing in the Hellenistic communities a fatal misrepresentation of Jesus, a betrayal of his ideals, and their replacement by alien concepts and aspirations."[29]

Further, according to the Acts of the Apostles Paul founded the Christian church at Philippi, having first gone on the Sabbath eve to the "Jewish place of prayer" (Acts 16:13), where those who first came to believe in Yeshua were assembled. Naturally the persons he met there were either Jews or gentile "fellow-travelers," that is, gentiles who were attracted to the Jewish tradition and way of life—known in the Acts as "God-fearers" or "God-worshippers" or simply "Greeks." Thus it was these two groups that comprised the great bulk of the first Christian churches outside Palestine, including the one that Paul founded and wrote to at Philippi and that met at the house of the God-worshipper Lydia. Hence, Paul's words must be understood as coming from a strict Jew to prayerful Jews or pious gentiles who were knowledgeable in and committed to the Bible and Judaism. With that in mind, let us look again at the pertinent part of the hymn:

> Your attitude must be that of Christ Jesus.
> Though he was in the form of God,
> he did not deem equality with God
> something to be grasped at.
> Rather, he emptied himself
> and took the form of a slave,
> being born in the likeness of human beings....
> Because of this God exalted him....

Many careful exegetes today see an "Adam Christology," which was so prevalent at the time Paul wrote, operating here. Being "in the form of God" simply means the same thing as Adam being "in the image of God," (Genesis 1:26), and that rather than "grasp at" that level of being, that is, at "equality with God," before the Fall (which came about because Adam wanted to "grasp at" being "as God"—Genesis 3:5), Yeshua chose to follow completely the path of Adam so as to redeem him, humbling himself and taking the "form of a slave" (Adam after the Fall)—completing in the poem the symmetry that is always present in Hebrew poetry. Toward the end of the poem God (not a person of the Trinity, but simply, "God," *ho theos*) "exalted," not "restored," him; Christ did not "retake" his allegedly former divine place. Jesus Christ here clearly is for the Jew Paul and his Jewish and semi-Jewish readers the "second Adam," not the pre-existent "second person" of the Trinity.[30]

## 10. Logos Theology

And what of the Prologue to John's Gospel where it says, "In the beginning was the Word, and the Word was with God, and the Word was God.... and the Word became flesh" (Jn 1:1,14)? Again, keeping in mind that this is a Jew writing largely for fellow Jews, it must be recalled that there were several figures and images used in biblical and early Jewish writings as *literary images* of the invisible God as made perceivable to humans. There is the Spirit of God who already in Genesis 1:1 moves over the darkness in creation, and Wisdom who is present at creation (Prov. 8:22f.; Ben Sira 24:9). In fact many scholars see the Prologue of John's Gospel as being originally largely a hymn to Wisdom with the

Word, and Yeshua, being substituted for Wisdom. When a comparison between the Prologue and a summary of the role of Wisdom as found in
Hebraic writings is made, the connection is apparent:

> Wisdom was created by God in the beginning; hidden with God
> and dwelling in the heavens; wisdom was present at the Creation,
> in which she served as agent (or instrument); she came to earth,
> sent to call both Israel and all humankind, some of whom listened
> to her, but most of whom did not; rejected by humanity and find-
> ing no place of rest, she returned to dwell with God.[31]

There is also the image of God's Word who in numerous biblical
(*dabar*, Hebrew) and post-biblical (*memra*, Aramaic) texts expresses God
to humanity, as does God's *Torah* (teaching) in both biblical and post-biblical texts, as well as God's Presence (*shekhinah*) in post-biblical Jewish
materials. It is within the context of this plethora of Jewish imagery of
God's visible side turned toward humanity that John wrote and his Jewish
readers understood him. But these were all metaphors, not ontological
substances, and that was likewise true of John's *logos,* the Word (*dabar,
memra*).

For the Jews the word of God was God speaking: God spoke and the
world was created. The Torah was God's word—indeed the ten com-
mand-ments, the deca-logue, means God's "ten words." God spoke to Israel through the prophets for hundreds of years. In short, the whole Jewish
experience of God was God speaking, expressing self, offering self for a
relationship with human beings. "This self-expression of God had been
going on for a long time before Jesus. It went back as far as humankind
could remember. It seemed that God had always been speaking, from the
beginning of the world."[32] Thus, as with Wisdom and the Spirit, it
seemed to the Jews that the Word had been with God from the beginning,
indeed again like Wisdom and Spirit, was God as perceived by humanity;
it "expressed God's own selfhood, and the one who encountered the word
encountered God."[33]

And why did those ancient Jews see Yeshua as God's Word become
flesh? Because their experience of Yeshua was that he was a diaphany of
God:

> Everything God has ever said is summed up in Jesus. It is all
> said there, every word. Not only are the teachings of Moses and
> the prophets summarized in the teaching of Jesus, everything God
> wants to reveal about who God is is shown in who Jesus is for us.
> Jesus is not just someone who has occasional words to say to us
> on God's behalf. He is in all the dimensions of his life God's

self-revelation. Thus the word of God was enfleshed in a human life.... This is the Johannine vision as scholars reconstruct it today.[34]

## 11. Dialogue Suggests a Resolution

I would like here to offer a possible resolution to the seemingly intractable problem between Christians and non-Christians, and for the modern mind in general, over the Christian claim of the confluence of the human and the divine in *Yeshua ha Notzri* which has come out of interreligious dialogue. This dialogue was not, however, between Christianity and Judaism, but between Christianity and Buddhism.

As a result of his long dialogue with Buddhism, the Japanese Christian Katsumi Takizawa (1909-1984) distinguishes between what he terms the primary and the secondary contacts of God with the human self. The first contact is the unconditional fact that God is with each one of us, is the very ground of our selves. This "contact" is real even though we may be unaware of it. The second contact occurs when we are awakened to that primary fact, allowing "the self to live in conscious accord with the will of God."[35]

According to Takizawa, Jesus was a man who was awakened to the primary fact—that is, he attained the secondary contact, and he did this so thoroughly and completely that he became a model for other selves.... Jesus was the person who in Hebrew tradition played the same role as did Gautama Buddha in the Indian tradition. The ground of salvation is the primary contact of God with the self, and this is the common ground of both Buddhism and Christianity.[36]

Utilizing this distinction, another Japanese Christian, Seiichi Yagi, analyzes the "I" in the words of Yeshua. He argues as follows: Yeshua at times speaks in a way that clearly indicates the distinction between himself and God and at other times in a way that indicates a unity between him and God. This occurs in various places in the several gospels, perhaps most clearly in John's Gospel. Yeshua speaks of the unity between him and God, whom he calls the Father: "That all may be one as you Father in me and I in you...that they may be one as we are one, I in them and you in me" (Jn 17: 21, 23); "Anyone who has seen me has seen the Father" (Jn 14:9); "Do you not believe that I am in the Father and the Father in me? The words I speak to you I do not speak of myself; but the Father who dwells in me does his works" (Jn 14:10). Here when Yeshua speaks it is fundamentally the Father speaking through him. The secondary contact has been so complete that it is the language of the unity between God the Father and Yeshua that comes forth. And yet there is a distinction between them for Yeshua obeys the Father when he says: "For I have not spoken of myself; but the Father who sent me gave me a commandment, what I should say, and what I should speak" (Jn 12:49).

> In John 14:10, Father and Son can be seen as two concentric circles in which the two centers coincide, whereas in John 12: 49, Father and Son appear as two centers in an ellipse, the latter obeying the former.... Christ is the Son of God insofar as the ultimate subject of the Son is the Father, but also insofar as the Father and the Son are distinguished from each other they are paradoxically one.[37]

Yagi goes on to note that these two types of relationship between Yeshua and God, the elliptic and the concentric, remind him of the two major kinds of Christologies in the ancient church, the Antiochocan and the Alexandrian. The Antiocheans (elliptic) maintained that there were two centers in the person of Yeshua, the divine and the human, and the latter obeyed the former. The Alexandrians (concentric) insisted that both centers coincided. "The ancient church, therefore, maintained that both christologies were true when, in the Council of Chalcedon, it declared that the divinity and the humanity of Christ were distinguishable but not separable."[38]

Such an explanation, I believe, makes sense out of the apparently conflicting language of the gospels and helps to make the reality that paradoxical language points to available to a contemporary person; if the Council of Chalcedon can be understood to be saying something of the same, it also helps to translate that Hellenistic ontological language into terms that likewise find resonance in a contemporary person's experience and thought patterns. It should be noticed, however, that the Yagi explanation is largely in psychological rather than abstract metaphysical terms. Further, what is said to be true in Yeshua's case, that the secondary contact with God (enlightenment, *satori*) in principle can happen to every human being. Indeed, Yeshua's language is full of exhortations to follow him, immitate him, be one with him and the Father.

Ultimately, of course, this explanation is not entirely different from the one I offered above when I wrote: Yeshua was so completely open to all dimensions of reality—as all human beings are in principle—that he was totally suffused with an inpouring of being in a "radical" way which included the "Root" of all being, God. Thus he was thoroughly human because he was through and through divine—which is evidenced in what he thought, taught and wrought. In fact, the perception by Richard Drummond of Yagi's understanding of Yeshua is expressed in very similar terminology: "Yagi sees the Jesus of history as one whose self had become transparent for the shining through (the working) of God as Ultimate Reality."[39]

## 12. "Divinization" in Religions

The dialogue between Christianity and Buddhism has something further to teach us Christians in the understanding of our Christologies. The "divinization" of the historical Yeshua into the transcendent Christ which occurred in Christianity as it moved from the Semitic cultural world into the Hellenistic was matched by a similar development with the "divinization" of the historical Siddharta Gautama into the transcendent Buddha ("Buddha," like "Christ," is not a proper name but a title; it means "the enlightened one") as it moved from the Indian cultural world into the Chinese and Far Eastern. Connected with this is the development from the "internal" understanding of "salvation" to the "external." This again is like the movement from the "teaching Yeshua" to the "proclaimed Christ," from the religion *of* Yeshua to the religion *about* Yeshua the Christ, from the "Yeshua of history" to the "Christ of faith."

These shifts are also in many ways paralleled in Buddhism with the movement from the "internal" understanding of "salvation" (termed *jiriki*, "self-power," in Japanese) to the "external" understanding (termed *tariki*, "other power"), from the "teaching Gautama" to the "proclaimed Buddha," from the religion *of* Gautama to the religion *about* Gautama the Buddha, from "the Gautama of history" (*Shakyamuni*) to the "Buddha of belief" (*Maitreya Buddha* and *Amida Buddha*).

Seeing the same kind of developments occurring in such disparate religious cultures (one even being theistic and the other originally non-theistic) should make Christians ask themselves what deeper grasping toward an underlying insight is represented by these "divinizing" moves, these moves which "ontologized" metaphorical language. Why did Christians, Buddhists, and others, make these moves? Perhaps one way to express the deeper insight that was sought is as follows:

For Christians Yeshua is the key figure through whom they get in touch with those dimensions of reality which go beyond, which transcend, the empirical, the everyday. This is fundamentally what Christologies are all about. All are attempts through the figure Yeshua to come into contact with the transcendent, the "divine," each Christology being perceived, conceived and expressed in its own cultural categories and images. Some do it better, even much better, than others; some do it even badly. Naturally they are all culture-bound. Otherwise they would not reflect and effectively speak to the people in that culture. But of course concommitantlly each Christology is proportionately limited in effectiveness in regard to other cultures, whether the cultural differences result from variations in geography, time, class, or whatever.

All Christians naturally can and should learn from the insights, and failures, of all other Christians' reaching out for the transcendent in their Christologies, and other theological reflections, but what is "religiously specific" about Christians is that these Christologies, these theological reflections, are, or at least should be, intimately connected and compatible with the person Yeshua of Nazareth—though of course (!) they are not limited to imitating him in cultural detail.

Thus, it should become clear to us Christians, and others, that in moving from talk about the "internal" to the "external," from the human to the divine, from Yeshua to Christ, we, like the Buddhists, and others, are attempting to express an experienced reality that transcends our every-day human experience, and hence also our every-day human language—limit-experience and limit-language, in the terminology of David Tracy.[40] We assert that there is a deeper reality which goes beyond the empirical surface experiences of our lives, and for us Yeshua is the bond-bursting means to become aware of that deeper reality (as for Buddhists it is Gautama). For us Christians it is preeminently in Yeshua that we encounter the divine, and therefore our move to talk about the divine in Yeshua. Hence, our attempt to speak of the divine in Yeshua, of Christ, etc., is not a mistake, but rather the result of the need to try to give expression to transempirical reality.

At the same time, however, we must be aware that when we attempt to speak of the transcendent we naturally will have to use transempirical language, that is, metaphor, symbol and the like. The mistake we must be cautious to avoid in this situation is erroneously to think that when we speak about the transcendent that we are using empirical language. We are not. We can not. At the same time we must also be cautious to avoid being reductionistic and erroneously think all talk about the transcendent is merely fantasizing, that since Yeshua was merely a human being and all later talk about the divine in him, etc., is simply romantic emoting with no referent in reality.

As I have argued, the "ontologization" move in language, that is, the "divinization" move, in fact is a response to an experienced profound reality. It should not be dismissed, but held onto for the vital insight into the meaning of human life it strives for—but it must be correctly understood for what it is, lest it become an idol, an image falsely adored, rather than the Reality toward which it points. When it is thus correctly understood and affirmed we will then have reached what Paul Ricoeur calls the "second naïveté," that is, the state of awareness in which the affirmation of the symbol, understood correctly for what it is, further unlocks for us the deeper, trans-empirical reality.

If this line of thought, prompted by seeing the parallels in "ontologization," "divinization," in Christianity and Buddhism, has any validity in explaining how Christians are coming to understand their Christologies, then many of the disagreements between Christians and Jews, Muslims and others in this area will disappear. Jews, Muslims and other religious persons will not thereby become Christians, of course, for Yeshua for them is not the door to the divine that he is for Christians, but perhaps their charges of blasphemy and idolatry against Christians will thereby be dissipated. But most important, the Christian tradition will thereby much more likely "make sense" to many contemporary Christians.

In sum, it must be asked: What does the Christian do about all the Christian traditions and doctrines that speak of Jesus Christ as God, the second person of the Blessed Trinity? Of course, as argued, they are not to be just dismissed; however, they are also not to be merely repeated with no further reflection either: simply to parrot the past is to pervert it. They must be taken with utmost seriousness, analyzed for the kind of language they are, and what reality they seek to express; they must be wrestled with and translated into our own contemporary thought categories. This is a huge task which has only been begun—and a few suggestions for which I have offered here.

As such a reconceptualization of Christian doctrines, especially Christology, into contemporary thought categories takes place—and it is taking place—it is to be expected that it will, of course, often meet with great resistance, as always happens with any major thought paradigm shift. Nevertheless, in carrying out this task, it should be remembered that if it has been held appropriate by the great bulk of Christian scholars and church authorities to apply the historical-critical and other contemporary critical methods to the Scriptures, said to be the word of God—and it has—*a fortiori* it is appropriate to apply the same methods to authoritative church statements and doctrines, which are *not* held to be the word of God. The same exegetical process must be engaged in in order to learn the "good news" handed on through the medium of the thought categories of an earlier age.

## 13. An Excursus: The Resurrection

Interreligious and intercultural dialogue and study suggest some other possible insights into a number of Christian mysteries that have long been mysterious to non-Christians, and doubtless many Christians as well. I would like to reflect here on just one that does not fit directly in the logic of this discussion, but that is nevertheless germane to it, namely, the Resurrection. I do not intend to undertake an extensive reflection on this Christian doctrine, but rather I simply wish to indicate possible help in understanding the doctrine that emerges from noticing that something similar goes on in other religious traditions.

Every culture develops a set of values and in the process comes to hold certain things in highest regard. For example, in the Greco-Roman religious culture there is a strong strain of body-spirit dualism; and of the two elements, body is definitely not as good as spirit. In fact, in some popular versions one might summarize the attitude as, "body bad, spirit good." Thus, for Plato the world of the Ideas was the real and the world of matter and the senses was shadowy—like the shadows on the wall of the cave (sense objects) with the bonfire (God) on the outside shinning on various figures (Ideas) and casting the shadows. For most in the Greco-Roman culture the body was like a jail which temporarily imprisoned the soul. As a consequence the Greeks developed the notion of the immortality, not of the body, but of the soul. Thus, the best one could say of someone who was highly valued was to say that her/his *spirit* lives on; s/he is immortalized, or indeed even "divinized," as were the Roman emperors.

In the Indian religious culture something similar, and yet different, was most highly valued. The individual spirit, self, *atman*, was seen as coming from the great world spirit, *Atman, or Brahman.* But each *atman* was caught in an ongoing circle of re-immersion into matter, the *samsara* circle of re-incarnation according to the deserts of the previous incarnation. The best that could happen is that the *samsaric* circle would be broken so that the individual *atman* could be freed (*moksha*) to re-merge with *Atman.*

The Indian Buddhist variation was that the *samsaric* circle of re-incarnation would be broken by *nirvana,* the "blowing out" of the false self, false *atman,* which let free the true spirit, self or *atman,* called the non-(false) self, the *anatman.* Thus, it was said that Gautama Buddha attained *nirvana* or *anatman.*

The Semitic religious culture held a much different understanding and resultant set of values in regard to the make-up of the human being. For them the human was much more non-dual. The human was not made up of two parts, matter and spirit, body and soul, which were radically separate from each other with one forced to exist temporarily in the other. Rather, the human was an integrated whole, a body-spirit, an ensouled-body, an embodied-spirit. Hence, eventually in the Hebraic-Judaic tradition there was developed by the Pharisees the notion of the resurrection of the body, the re-enspiriting, the re-animating of the body. Thus, in the Judaic tradition all humans were expected to rise once again, bodily re-enspirited, at the end of days. Again, the most exciting thing that Yeshua could do was to raise someone from the dead, as he was reported to have done several times. Hence, the best thing that could have been said of Yeshua in the Judaic religious culture was that he was bodily raised from the dead.

No Hindu would ever have thought of saying that one of their holy men or women have, or should, come back bodily from the dead; nor would any Buddhist ever have thought of saying that Gautama Buddha has risen, or should rise, bodily from the dead. That would have been saying the worst of them, who were the best; it would have been re-condemning them to the *samsaric* circle of the re-incarnational immersions in matter.

Similarly, no Greek would ever have thought of saying of Socrates, or Plato, that they were raised from the dead, or ought to be, or hoped to be. That would have been wishing the worst, not the best, for Socrates or Plato. It would have been wishing their immortal spirits back into their corruptible material bodies, back into the prisons they had escaped from. But that is precisely what the Jews prized most highly: "The trumpet shall sound, and the dead shall rise!" Hence, that is also exactly what some Jews said of Yeshua: He was bodily raised from the dead.

Recall, however, the incredulous, scornful reaction of the Greeks of Athens when they heard Paul speak of Yeshua's being raised from the dead. At first they said, "We would like to know this new teaching that you are talking about." They listened patiently until Paul got to the part where he said, "'He [God] has given proof of this to everyone by raising that man [Yeshua] from death!' When they heard Paul speak about a raising from death, some of them made fun of him" (Acts 17: 31f.).

These four different religious cultures all say the best about their best, but that first best turns out to be different for each religious culture. That fact suggests that the fundamental message in each instance is not primarily immortality, *moksha, nirvana* or resurrection. Rather, the primary message is that those persons have attained the best, the highest in their religious culture, and therefore the best is predicated of them. Whether Socrates' spirit has attained immortality, or Gautama attained *nirvana*, Yeshua has been bodily raised from the dead is not the most fundamental point of each claim—after all, none of them can be "proved," but only accepted on some kind of faith or trust, which of course may well have a reasonable, but not ineluctably persuasive, basis. The most fundamental point of each claim is that each person is held up as a preeminently lived model of how one should live an authentic, a fully human, a (w)holy life—and this is "rewarded" and attested to by their crowning achievement: whether immortality, *moksha, nirvana,* or resurrection.

## 14. Conclusion

Yeshua, Jesus, is the measure, the standard, of what it means to be Christian. His followers, who are now called Christians, look to that historical figure who was a Jew living in Israel two thousand years ago as the model of how to live a full, whole, holy human life, a life that is open to all reality and the Source of reality; his followers see the Source of all reality, God, self-disclosed in the most complete manner possible in this human being, Yeshua the Jew. Every perceiver of reality necessarily sees reality only partially, from her or his perspective. Hence, all perceptions of, all reactions to, all doctrines about, Yeshua are also necessarily limited, seen from a particular perspective. Gathering them together, of course, can be immensely helpful in the task of gaining an ever fuller perception of Yeshua, but it is the historical Yeshua who Christians are seeking to know, and then follow as a model of how to lead a full human, divine-disclosing, life.

The doctrines of the divinity of Christ are important attempts to express and transmit in particular cultural thought categories the human encounter with the transcendent, but they are necessarily cast in transempirical, metaphorical language and thought categories. They must be understood, and appreciated, as such, so they can assist Christians to live whole, holy, human, divine-disclosing lives—in imitation of Yeshua.

## Notes

1. See "Iesous" in Gerhard Kittel, ed., *Theological Dictionary of the New Testament* (Grand Rapids, MI: Eerdmans, 1966), vol. III, pp. 284ff.
2. Where the root meaning of the Indo-European words for salvation is fullness, wholeness, the root meaning of the Semitic word used here, "shua," is that of capaciousness, openness. Salvation then means the opposite of being in straits; it means being free in wide open space. This makes it close to, though not precisely the same as, the Indo-European root meaning.
3. The Jewish scholar Geza Vermes confirms this Semitic understanding of salvation as being current with Yeshua and his contemporaries when he points out that they linked together physical and spiritual health: "In the somewhat elastic, but extraordinarily perceptive religious terminology of Jesus and the spiritual men of his age, 'to heal', 'to

expel demons' and 'to forgive sins' were interchangeable synonyms," *Jesus and the World of Judaism* (Philadelphia: Fortress Press, 1983), p. 10.

4. Cf. Eduard Schweizer, *Jesus Christus* (Hamburg, 1972), pp. 19f.; Ernst Käsemann, *Das Problem des historischen Jesus—exegetische Besinnungen*, vol. 1 (Göttingen, 1960), pp. 187, 205. The Professor of New Testament at the Protestant faculty of the University of Bern, Switzerland, Ulrich Luz, makes the point even more sharply: "Not only did Jesus not declare himself to his people as the Messiah; more than likely he did not even consider himself to be the Messiah," in Pinchas Lapide & Ulrich Luz, *Jesus in Two Perspectives* (Minneapolis: Augsburg, 1985), p. 129.

5. Hans Küng, *Christentum und Weltreligionen* (Munich: Piper, 1984), p. 451.

6. E. P. Sanders, *Jesus and Judaism* (Philadelphia: Fortress, 1985), p. 2.

7. Geza Vermes, *Jesus and the World of Judaism* (Philadelphia: Fortress, 1983), p. 81.

8. This position is taken by Küng, Schillebeeckx and many other prominent Catholic and Protestant theologians; see Leonard Swidler, ed., *Consensus in Theology?* (Philadelphia: Westminster Press, 1980). E.g., Hans Küng:

> And for the Catholic Christian too this criterion can be nothing but the Christian message, the *Gospel* in its ultimate concrete form, *Jesus Christ, himself*, who for the Church and—despite all assertions to the contrary—also for me is the Son and Word of God. He is and remains the norm in the light of which every ecclesiastical authority—which is not disputed—must be judged: the norm by which the theologian must be tested and in the light of which s/he must continually justify her/himself in the spirit of self-criticism and true humility (p. 163).

The Protestant theologian Ulrich Luz made the same point abundantly clear when he wrote:

> *Christianity must appeal to Jesus if it wants to endure* without allowing itself to be transformed willy-nilly by anyone and by every historical epoch. It *must* appeal to Jesus, as long as it continues to affirm that God acted historically in Jesus and not merely in our momentary faith experiences and ideas.

He added that he was "convinced that appealing to Jesus cannot be painless and without consequences for us in the present; rather, it demands that our churches modify their theology and practice." Lapide & Luz, *Jesus in Two Perspectives*, p. 159.

9. Edward Schillebeeckx, *Jesus* (New York: Seabury, 1979), p. 61. Schillebeeckx notes the distinction between the historical Yeshua and our apprehension of him and states that the former is the ultimate Christian norm: "It is not the historical image of Jesus, but the living Jesus of history who stands at the beginning and is the source, norm and criterion." He then argues that historical-critical research was the means by which the earliest "reactions to," i.e., the original Christian beliefs, measure up to the final standard, "the living Jesus of history": "historical critical research can clarify for us the Jesus of history." Edward Schillebeeckx, *Die Auferstehung Jesu als Grund der Erlösung* (Freiburg: Herder, 1978), p. 44. In other words, our apprehensions—by whatever methods (other critical methods also contribute to our fuller, deeper—and never endingly so—apprehension of the historical Yeshua, e.g., literary-critical and psychosocial-critical methods)—of the historical Yeshua will always fall short of apprehending him fully, but the very best "penultimate" image of the real historical Yeshua is the very best "temporary" final norm we can have for what is authentically Christian—until a fuller image of the historical Yeshua is developed, *ad infinitum*.

10. Schillebeeckx, *Jesus*, pp. 62.

11. Vermes, *Jesus and the World of Judaism*, p. 44.

12. Joseph G. Kelly, "Lucan Christology and the Jewish-Christian Dialogue," *Journal of Ecumenical Studies*, 21,4 (Fall, 1984), pp. 693, 704, 708.

13. Ivan Havener, *Q The Sayings of Jesus* (Wilmington: Michael Glazier, 1987), p. 11. Like Kelly, Havener is also a Catholic scholar.
14. Ibid.
15. Ibid., p. 71.
16. Ibid.
17. W. M. Thompson, *The Jesus Debate* (New York: Paulist, 1985), p. 10.
18. Cf. Gerd Theissen, *Sociology of Early Palestinian Christianity* (Philadelphia: Fortress Press, 1977), p. 83: "The Jesus movement found doors opened to them in the Hellenistic cities because they could offer prospects of a resolution of the tensions between Jews and Gentiles: theirs was a universalistic Judaism, which was open to outsiders."
19. Schillebeeckx, *Jesus*, p. 527.
20. Cf. Schweizer, *Jesus Christus*, pp. 19f., etc.
21. Paul Tillich made the same point when he wrote that the statement "God has become man" is not paradoxical but "nonsensical" because "it is a combination of words which makes sense only if it is not meant to mean what the words say. The word 'God' points to ultimate reality, and even the most consistent Scotists had to admit that the only thing God cannot do is to cease to be God. But that is just what the assertion that 'God has become man' means." Paul Tillich, *Systematic Theology* (Chicago: University of Chicago, 1957), vol. 2, p. 94.
22. A related idea about the genre of language used in various religious texts was stressed by Monika Hellwig in discussing the language of the Tome of Pope Leo the Great, which became so influential in the christological language of the Council of Chalcedon:

    > Throughout this document, Leo argues directly from the language of worship and piety to the abstract formulations that came to dominate the Council of Chalcedon. There is, of course, no reflection on the nature of religious language.... One is compelled to ask whether there may have been a misperception of literary genre. The poetic language of piety seems to be used as though it were a simple historical record of the already self-critically nuanced language of a systematic exposition.

    Monika Hellwig, "From the Jesus of Story to the Christ of Dogma," in Alan T. Davies, ed., *Antisemitism and the Foundations of Christianity* (New York: Paulist, 1979), p. 123.
23. The Dutch Catholic theologian Ansfried Hulsbosch—who unfortunately died at a relatively young age—took the evolutionary thought of Teilhard de Chardin seriously and developed an insightful Christology. He argued that the divinity of Yeshua consisted precisely in the perfection of his humanity. He wrote that Yeshua "is the Son of God in that this man is in contact with God in a way that separates Him from ordinary men. But this can mean nothing other than a special way of being-man, since the whole actuality of the mystery lies precisely in the sector of the human." He then added that, "The divine nature of Jesus is relevant to the saving mystery only insofar as it alters and elevates the human nature. And whatever that is, it must be called a new mode of being man." Ansfried Hulsbosch, "Jezus Christus, gekend als mens, beleden as Zoon Gods," *Tijdschrift voor Theologie*, 6 (1966), p. 255. It is summarized along with two other key articles from the same special number of the *Tijdschrift* by Piet Schoonenberg and Edward Schillebeeckx in the article "Soul-Body Unity and God-Man Unity," by Robert North in *Theological Studies*, 30 (March, 1969), pp. 27-60; 36f.
24. Edward Schillebeeckx, "Persoonlijke openbaringsgestalte van de Vader," *Tijdschrift voor Theologie*, 6 (1966), pp. 276f. (North, "Soul-Body," pp. 40f.). Ulrich Luz underlines a similar point about the shift from the Jewish way of thinking to the Greek way and its impact on Christology. He writes that,

The confession of Jesus' divinity may have been unavoidable and quite pertinent for the Greeks and for Europeans of the previous centuries, whose thought processes had been shaped by Platonic metaphysics, even though the possibility of a conversation with Israel thereby became inevitably strained. However, this confession has always been problematic insofar as it has threatened to swallow the humanity of Jesus as well as the historical reality of his mission; theologically this is the case in its monophysite form, but for me this is also largely true of its Chalcedonian, non-Antiochene form. In my opinion it is impossible for us to go on thinking as the Greeks once did, even though we have learned, and still can learn, much from them. (Lapide & Luz, *Jesus in Two Perspectives*, p. 165.)

25. Jerome Murphy-O'Connor, O.P., argues in great detail that the common belief that Phil. 2:6-11 speaks of Christ's pre-existence as God and his subsequent incarnation is "a presupposition rather than conclusion" that is unwarranted. "Christological Anthropology in Phil. 2:6-11," *Revue Biblique*, 83 (1976), pp. 30ff. See also James D.G. Dunn, *Christology in the Making* (Philadelphia: Westminster, 1980), pp. 114ff.

26. Sanders, *Jesus*, p. 21.

27. Vermes, *Jesus and the World of Judaism*, p. 72.

28. James Barr, *Semantics of Biblical Language* (London, 1961), p. 250.

29. Vermes, *Jesus and the World of Judaism*, p. 26.

30. See ibid. and Thomas N. Hart, *To Know and Follow Jesus* (New York: Paulist Press, 1984), pp. 94ff.; Schillebeeckx, *Jesus;* Piet Schoonenberg, *The Christ* (New York: Seabury, 1971); Piet Schoonenberg, "'He Emptied Himself': Philippians 2:7," in *Who Is Jesus of Nazareth?*, *Concilium*, vol. 11 (New York: Paulist, 1965), pp. 47-66.

31. Havener, *Q The Sayings of Jesus, p. 78.*

32. Hart, *To Know and Follow Jesus*, p. 98.

33. Ibid.

34. Ibid., p. 99.

35. Seiichi Yagi, "'I' in the Words of Jesus," in Paul Knitter and John Hick, eds., *The Myth of Christian Uniqueness: Toward a Pluralistic Theology of Religions* (Maryknoll, NY: Orbis Books, 1987), p. 117. Yagi here summarizes this aspect of Takizawa's work and goes on to apply it Yeshua, and Paul with some additional help from the Zen Buddhist Shin-ichi Hisamatsu (1889-1980).

36. Ibid.

37. Ibid., pp. 121f.

38. Ibid., p. 122.

39. Richard H. Drummond, "Dialogue and Integration: the Theological Challenge of Yagi Seiichi," *Journal of Ecumenical Studies*, 24,4 (Fall, 1987), p. 569.

40. David Tracy, *Blessed Rage for Order* (New York: 1975), pp. 91 ff.

# CHAPTER 2

# Yeshua and His Followers Were Not Christians—They were Jews: Implications for Christians Today

## 1. Yeshua the Torah-true Jew

Christians have tended to portray Yeshua as having made the Law no longer binding, as having left the Law behind along with Judaism, both of which had a purpose in preparing the way for and bringing forth the Messiah. But then, since he had come, both were superseded. Judaism held onto the Law, and it led to death, whereas Christianity followed the gospel and grace, and it led to life. It was as if Kipling were anticipated: "Law is Law and gospel is gospel, and never the twain shall meet." It is with this club of the "death-dealing Law" that Christians have bludgeoned Jews since New Testament days. Hence it is vital to Christian self-knowledge, and to the relationship between the two religions, that the record be set straight on the attitude of Yeshua the "founder" of Christianity toward Law.

To begin, the one who Christians claim is the foundation, the cornerstone of their religion, is Jesus of Nazareth, *Yeshua ha Notzri*, who, it should be recalled was himself *not* a Christian. He was a Jew, a very observant Jew. That meant that Yeshua did not come to dispense with or do away with the Torah, the Law. He came to carry it out. It should also be remembered that although the Hebrew term Torah was translated by the Greek Septuagint as *nomos*, Law, Torah in fact has a much wider meaning, namely, "instruction," instruction on how to lead a proper, full Jewish, human, life. Thus, when the term *nomos* appears in the New Testament it almost invariably means Torah, although in some instances it might also include the "oral Torah," or *halakhah*—the rules of conduct as interpreted and derived from the written Torah by the rabbis, or proto-rabbis, including Yeshua.

The Hebrew term, *halakhah*, meaning the "way" or "walk," which in rabbinic writing comes to mean the decision on the correct way to act in a

33

specific case, does not as such turn up in the gospels, but the reality to which it refers is often recorded, that is, when Yeshua asserts that a particular way is how to apply the Torah in a life circumstance. It is interesting to notice, however, that the equivalent of *halakhah* in Greek, *hodos,* does appear in the Acts of the Apostles when describing the practices of the followers of Yeshua: "I worship the God of our fathers according to The Way (*hodos*)" (Acts 24:14). It is in this sense as a decision about the correct way to apply the Torah, God's instruction, to concrete life that Rabbi Phillip Sigal speaks of the *halakhah* of Yeshua—and I do the same here.

As stated, Yeshua was a Jew, and an observant one, that is, he was committed to the keeping of the Law in the way that seemed best to him. Since he was a "rabbi," he taught others to do likewise. In brief, he did not come to dispense with or do away with the Torah, the Law. He came to carry it out.

Such a blunt statement might well have been a shock to most past Christians, and many of them today, but it has the growing support of contemporary Christian and Jewish scholars. One Orthodox Israeli Jewish scholar, Pinchas Lapide, said of Yeshua that he "never and nowhere broke the Law of Moses, the Torah of Moses, nor did he in any way provoke its infringement—it is entirely false to say that he did.... This Jesus was as faithful to the Law as I would hope to be. I even suspect that Jesus was more faithful to the Law than I am—and I am an Orthodox Jew."[1]

The Catholic New Testament scholar Franz Mussner argues that one should not read the Yeshua tradition in the gospels *a priori* in the light of the Pauline justification teaching, which grew out of the reflection on the saving significance of the death and resurrection of Yeshua. Rather, one should not hesitate to view the affirmation of the Law in Mt. 5:19 (Lk. 16:17) as coming from Yeshua. Indeed, "The Jewishness of Jesus is especially reflected in it."[2]

Another Israeli Orthodox Jewish scholar put the matter this way: Yeshua was "a Torah-true Jew,"[3] as did also another: "Jesus remained steadfast to the old *Torah:* till his dying day he continued to observe the ceremonial laws like a true Pharisaic Jew."[4] A Jewish professor of rabbinics at Cambridge University stated the same idea: "Nor can I accept that Jesus' purpose was to do away with Judaism as he found it. He had his criticisms, to be sure, but he wanted to perfect the law of Moses, not to annul it. The Christian hostility to this law strikes me as a betrayal of Jesus' teaching."[5] The scholar of judaistics Johann Maier made the same point:

There is no evidence that Jesus had intended a suspension of the Torah. Rather, he was perceived as so devout that the Pharisees even displayed a positive interest in him and viewed him as worthy of travelling around with. Likewise, the Jewish-Christian community saw no reason to give up the Torah either in theory or practice.... In no individual concrete case—either in relation to the Sabbath healing, or in ritual purity practice, or in the question of divorce—is there a fundamental conflict with "the Law."[6]

The Protestant New Testament scholar Julius Wellhausen was equally strong when insisting that Yeshua was not a Christian, but a Jew: "He did not preach a new faith, but taught humans to do the will of God; and in his opinion, as also in that of the Jews, the will of God was to be found in the Law and in the other books of Scripture."[7] The contemporary Protestant exegete E. P. Sanders cooly rejects the view that Yeshua broke the Law: "Opinions range from this extreme all the way to another: there is no violation of the law at all or none worth much mention. In this case, one of the extremes must be judged to be correct: the second one."[8]

These and other recent scholars argue strongly that those Christians who attempt to set up some sort of dichotomy between the Law and grace, as if Judaism were a religion only of Law and Christianity were a religion only of gospel, of grace—whatever else they might be, in this regard they are not followers of Yeshua. He at any rate was committed to the keeping of the Law, the Torah, "as long as heaven and earth last!" and "whoever breaks even the smallest of the commandments, and teaches others to do the same, will be least in the Reign of heaven" (Mt. 5:18f.). There was no notion whatsoever of the abolishment of the Law in his words: "Do not think that I came to destroy the Law or the prophets; I came not to destroy but to carry out" (*plerosai*, literally, to implement; Mt. 5:17-19).[9]

The same is true of the variant claim that Judaism is a religion of law and justice but that Christianity is a religion of love. Yeshua made it clear that there was no split between the two. Rather, they were one. He summed up his understanding of religion as the following of the twofold command or law: to love God and neighbor. This, of course, was nothing new. He was simply quoting from the ancient Torah, Deut. 6:5, indeed, a portion of the opening of the Jewish daily prayer, the *Shema:* "Love the Lord your God with all your heart, with all your soul, and with all your strength," and Lev. 19:18: "Love your neighbor as you love yourself." In fact, the linking together of these two commandments and the summing up of the Law in them was not something new or special to Yeshua. According to Luke 10:25-28, it was an "expert in the law" in the crowd who spoke of the twofold command of love; Yeshua merely agreed with him. Moreover, perhaps two hundred years before Yeshua was born other Jewish writers stated much the same sentiments. They are found in various of the Pseudepigrapha (non-canonical Jewish writings in Greek): "Love the Lord and the neighbor" (*Testament of Issachar* 5:2); "I loved the Lord and every human being with my whole heart" (ibid., 7:6); "Love the Lord in your whole life and one another with a sincere heart" (*Testament of Daniel* 5:3); "Fear the Lord and love the neighbor" (*Testament of Benjamin* 3:3); "And he commanded them to keep to the way of God, do justice, and everyone love his/her neighbor" (*Jubilees* 20:9); "Love one another my sons as brothers, as one loves oneself.... You should love one another as yourselves" (ibid., 36:4-6).

Precisely the same summing up of the Law, Torah, in the double commandment of love was expressed by a Jewish contemporary of Yeshua, Philo of Alexandria (c. 20 B.C.E.-50 C.E.). In the tractate, "Concerning Individual Commandments," II,63, he wrote: "There are, so to speak, two fundamental teachings to which the numberless individual teachings and statements are subordinated: in reference to God the commandment of honoring God and piety, in reference to humanity that of the love of humanity and justice."

Phillip Sigal notes that "The rabbi par excellence of the first century, Akiba, far from denying that the love command is a significant criterion by which all action should be measured, insisted upon it," and gives the rabbinic references, as well as several other supporting rabbinical citations in addition to those given above.[10]

In sum: these are not the words of a religion that is defective in love. Yeshua did indeed stress Torah and love—and in this he stressed the Jewish tradition.

And what of those who proffer the other variation of the same theme which would make of Christianity a religion that was concerned not with works but with faith, with "faith alone," and Judaism a religion of "works righteousness"? Whatever they are, in this they are not followers of Yeshua. According to him, those who are saved, who will enter into the reign of God are not those who claim they have faith, who cry out "Lord, Lord!" but those who *do* corporal works of mercy: who feed the hungry, clothe the naked, house the homeless, care for the sick and imprisoned. According to Matthew, Yeshua commended the good saying: "For I was hungry and you gave me food; I was thirsty and you gave me drink; I was a stranger and you made me welcome; naked and you clothed me, sick and you visited me, in prison and you came to see me," (Mt. 25: 35-36). However, this is paralleled both in the earlier Hebrew Bible and in later rabbinic writings: R. Hama son of R. Hanina (3rd century Palestinian rabbi) said one should imitate God, "as he clothes the naked...(Gen. 3:21) so you too must clothe the naked. The Holy One...visited the sick...(Gen. 18:1), so you too must visit the sick. The Holy One...comforted the mourners...(Gen. 25:11), so you too must comfort the mourners. The Holy One...buried the dead...(Dt. 34:6), so you too must bury the dead."[11]

James (in Hebrew, Jacob) wrote: "Faith without works is dead" (Jas. 2:17). It should be noted, however, that the teaching of Yeshua and Jacob is not a polarizing "either-or" but a comprehensive "both-and." "His faith and his actions worked together" (Jas. 2:22). This is ancient Jewish teaching, as is exemplified in the words of the prophet Habakkuk: "The just *live* by faith" (Hab. 2:4). Both faith, *emunah,* trust in God, and the works that naturally flow from this sustaining trust and commitment are what characterize the just man and woman, the Jew, and hence also the follower of Yeshua.

In brief, Yeshua, as a faithful Jew, was committed to affirming and keeping the Torah.

Much like Hillel and Shammai before him, Yeshua developed his own way of how to interpret and apply the Torah to life—not at all a simple matter, as the dozens of volumes of the Talmud indicate. A great deal of Yeshua's Torah interpretation, his *halakhot,* can be found imbedded in the gospels, though perhaps often in redacted form—though so are the other rabbis' *halakhot* redacted in the Talmud. In thus interpreting and applying the Torah Yeshua followed good rabbinic practice, and in no way thereby moved outside Judaism, despite what might be considered by some Jews his "liberal" handling of the Torah—in this he was much more like Hillel than Shammai.

The writer of our version of the gospel according to Matthew wrote perhaps around 85 C.E. with great polemic against the Pharisees (and probably also the post-70 rabbis) and their emphasis on the Torah, *halakhah.* He had, therefore, every reason to neglect, suppress, significantly change or at least nuance Yeshua's strong commitment, quoted above (Mt. 5:17-19), to the keeping of the Torah. But he did not. Apparently the Yeshuanic tradition of adhering to the Torah was still so strong more than half a century after the death of Yeshua that he did not dare distort it. No matter how "liberal" an interpretation of the Torah Yeshua may have been perceived as teaching in order to fulfill "the spirit" rather than just "the letter" of the Torah (as Paul expressed it: "in the spirit, not in the letter," Rom. 2:29) it is undeniable that he was immovably firm on the "carrying out" of all of the Torah—till the end of the world.[12]

Another argument, perhaps the most definitive, that Yeshua had not stood in opposition to the Torah was put forth by one of the few Christian New Testament scholars who know the Jewish materials, including the rabbinic, first hand, E. P. Sanders. As we know from the New Testament, from the very beginning, immediately after the passion and resurrection events, the Jewish followers of Yeshua were expected to continue to follow the Torah, and did; whether the gentile followers who came later were or not was the subject of a great dispute between Peter and Paul and others—both facts clear proof that Yeshua had *not* in his lifetime signaled opposition to the Torah. In explaining the fact that sometimes Yeshua took a more stringent stand than that required by a passage in the Torah— e.g., regarding the divorce of women by men—Sanders speaks of Yeshua's affirming the Torah and moving beyond it, and in that limited, negative sense finding it not adequate.[13]

The Catholic New Testament scholar Franz Mussner has an enlightening remark in this regard:

> One could describe Jesus of Nazareth, precisely in what concerns his understanding of the "fulfilling" of the Law, as a "Reform Jew," but of course as the most influential and most radical Reform Jew Judaism has ever produced. There has, however, always been a place for a "Reform Judaism" within Judaism. With his criticism concerning the concrete realization of the life according to the Law Jesus has not fallen outside the framework of Judaism—as precisely the Jewish scholars of the life of Jesus emphasize.[14]

In dealing with the Law, the Torah, Yeshua of course had to apply it to everyday life, he had to fashion concrete rules of conduct, that is, *halakhot.* He was, as Phillip Sigal phrased it, "a proto-rabbinic halakhist as well as a charismatic prophet."[15] If he applied the Law to concrete life, it would, of course, be apparent that Yeshua was in favor of the Law. But a traditional Christian manuever here has been to point out that he abrogated parts of the Law, indeed even the written Torah—something a rabbi would never do. However, as Phillip Sigal points out, "the abrogation of specific precepts of the written Torah is not unsual for Jesus' milieu," and notes that the tannaitic rabbi R. Nathan stated that when "one must act for the Lord, annulment of provisions is allowed. He maintains this in reference to either Torah, the written or the interpretative...no 'law' is absolute. What stands above all is the will of God,"[16] which is applied through the interpretative wisdom of the rabbi. One example of many of such rabbinic abrogations of parts of the written Torah is the recinding of the trial by ordeal of the suspected adulterous wife (Num. 5:11-31) by the contemporary of Yeshua, Rabbi Yohanan ben Zakkai.[17]

A frequent example offered by Christian scholars of Yeshua's "sovereign abrogation" of a central written Torah obligation which supposedly set him outside the rabbinic tradition is Yeshua's statement found in Mark 2:27: "The sabbath was made for human beings, not human beings for the sabbath." However, a very close paraphrase is also found in an early rabbinic writing: "The sabbath is commited to you; you are not committed to the sabbath" (*Mekilta* 31:13). In fact, Sigal argues that, "During his brief ministry Jesus was a proto-rabbi whose views influenced his contemporaries and possibly entered tannaitic literature as the views of others.... A classic example of a view enunciated by Jesus which is attributed to later tanna R. Simon B. Menasia" is the Mekilta statement about the sabbath.[18] Either way, Yeshua in this regard was in the center of the rabbinic tradition—either as being paralleled or plagiarized.

Sometimes almost in desperation to make Yeshua different, to separate him from Judaism, Christian scholars point out that a number of times Yeshua cites the Torah and then says, "but I say to you," arguing that as an ordinary rabbi he could not do such a thing in contradiction to the word of God; he therefore must have divine sovereignty over the Torah. Again, a lack of knowledge of the rabbinic materials has betrayed such Christian scholars. Language of this sort by Yeshua "should not be regarded as evidence of anything more than proto-rabbinic insistence upon one's own view even when it contradicts and abolishes earlier teaching. It is found used by the first-second century sage, R. Simon b. Yohai, at T. Sot. 6:6-11.... It is self-evident that people 'marvelled' at Menahem b. Sungai (T. Ed.3:1) as they did at Jesus (Mt. 7:28)."[19] Elsewhere Sigal states clearly:

> A major characteristic of this proto-rabbinic development, however, was the assumption of religious authority by individuals. These individuals, by force of personality and learning, were capable of changing previous halakha, unsettling tradition and inaugurating new trends.... It is this diversity which in great measure is the key to our understanding of the Matthean Jesus.[20]

Thus, far from being different because of his strong teaching style in regard to Torah, Yeshua fitted very well into his intellectual and cultural environment on its account. Later, of course, after 70 C.E., the custom developed of deciding on the correct way, the *halakhah,* by a majority vote among the rabbis—but that was not yet the case before 70 when Yeshua taught.

An excellent example of someone else who was a strong teacher of Torah, one who could also abrogate the written Torah, e.g., the *sotah* trial of a suspected adulteress, was Yeshua's contemporary Yohanan ben Zakkai. He spent twenty years in Galilee, studied with Hillel and Shammai, was a forceful, independent and original thinker, and in a significant way "founded" a new religion, or rather, forged a new direction in Judaism, "Rabbinic Judaism"—in all this both Yohanan and Yeshua were much alike. As Sigal has speculated with warrant that, given all the time Yohanan spent in the small area of Galilee, his interests, and his similarity in thought to that of Yeshua, the chances are high they knew each other, were quite possibly first fellow students of the school of Hillel and Shammai and then colleagues, and hence could very well have held halakhic discussions together. Moreover, when it is recalled that Yohanan ben Zakkai became the leader of the Hillelite school—to which Yeshua was in many regards very close—and made that interpretation of Torah dominant in all subsequent Judaism, it would seem to make much more sense to view Yeshua as very much "in" rather than "out" of the mainstream of pre-70 Judaism.

Geza Vermes noted the striking similarity between Yeshua and the Qumran Teacher of Righteousness: Like Yeshua, "The Teacher of Righteousness...served as transmitter and interpreter of the divine mysteries, of God's definitive revelation. Like Jesus, he was surrounded by faithful disciples who continued to adhere to, and practise, his doctrines after his death.... Like Jesus' followers, they organized themselves into a separate, self-contained body of the chosen, some of them living like the Jesusalem church out of a common purse and shunning private ownership of property." However, unlike the Qumran sectaries, who "closed the doors of their community to all except Jews,"[21] the followers of Yeshua, after much soul-searching, decided to admit non-Jews to their company without first becoming Jews.

What then was special about the teaching of Yeshua? Was there anything at all special? As seen before, the great commandments of love were already there in the Judaic heritage. The notion of freedom from the Law was something that Paul, not Yeshua, expressed (and then only for the gentile followers of Yeshua, not the Jewish; see Romans 9-11). Of course, there was something special about the teaching of Yeshua. First of all, the specific extraordinary constellation of teachings is a mark of the creative genius of Yeshua. As the Jewish New Testament scholar David Flusser has pointed out, although one may fundamentally be able to reproduce the gospel out of citations from the many volumes of rabbinic writings, one would first have to have the gospels before one in order to do it. Further, as noted, given the fact that the interpretation and application of the Torah was greatly in flux at the time of Yeshua, his own interpretation "according to the spirit" was just that, his own, even though it lay in the direction of his great predecessor, Hillel.

However, Yeshua was not satisfied with teaching that the whole of the Torah should be carried out according to its spirit. He went beyond it in holding out the ideal of a self-emptying (kenotic, as Paul said in Phil. 2:6) love for one's friends, one's neighbors, even one's enemies—as seen especially in the Sermon on the Mount (Mt. 5ff.). The Rabbis had a phrase for halachic decisions which went beyond the demands of the Torah, *lifnim meshurat hadin* ("beyond the requirements of the court"): "Proto-rabbis sometimes encouraged going beyond the strict requirement of law or the literal reading of a text. In this way they inspired some to sacrifice their monetary or property right under law in order to extend equity to others. This is how we are to understand Mt. 5:40 ["And if anyone sue you at law and take away your coat, let him have your cloke as well."]."[22]

However, what was most special about Yeshua was that he *lived* not only according to the Torah, but also according to his supererogatory kenotic ideal, *lifnim meshurat hadin*—even to the point of agonizingly dying for the sake of his friends: "Greater love than this has no one, but that he gives his life for his friends" (that is, for "those loved by him," Jn. 15:13). As Geza Vermes put it, "the heart of Jesus' message" was its "stress on interiority and supererogation."[23]

Thus, what apparently struck many of Yeshua's contemporaries about him and made them his disciples must have been his inner wisdom and love, which shone through his teaching the fulfillment of the whole Torah according to its spirit. He presented an ideal of kenotic love that went beyond it, and lived and died accordingly in his *whole* person. What Yeshua "thought, taught, and wrought," that whole, that life (and death), is what made Yeshua special—for many, a human transparency of the divine.

Clearly for Yeshua it was not a question of living by the Law, the Torah, *or* the spirit, but rather, by living (and dying) the whole Law (Torah) according to its spirit, he thought, taught and wrought a life that was open to and showed forth the Source and Goal of the Torah—YHWH: "Be perfect as my heavenly Father is perfect." Not freedom *from* the Law but freedom *through* the Law *and beyond* to kenotic love, *lifnim meshurat hadin*. Augustine put it: "Love, and do what you will," "*Ama, et fac quod vis,*" for your love will lead you not contrary to the Law, but to it, and beyond.

Still, the living and dying according to the Torah and beyond did not in any way place Yeshua outside of Judaism. The Rabbis described this kenotic love with the biblical term *hesed,* often simply translated as "loving kindness." A *hasid* is one who's life is centered on *hesed,* i.e., one whose philosophy of life is not to be "content with minimum standard of conduct but to go beyond the letter of the law."[24] Thus, as Yeshua urged his followers to be "perfect as your heavenly Father is perfect," so the later Rabbis often described God as practicing *hesed,* as being a *hasid.*[25] In advocating living in kenotic love, in *hesed,* Yeshua also spoke of living in the spirit, of sending the holy spirit, and urged others to learn from his humility. Note the following striking Rabbinic parallels. "A life led in the spirit of *hesed* was, moreover, thought to be the harbinger of the holy spirit (*Shekalim* 9b)."[26] "Holiness leads to humility; humility to the fear of sin; the fear of sin to the holy spirit; the holy spirit to the resurrection of the dead. But *hasiduth* [the practice of *hesed*] is greater than all these!"[27] A contemporary Jewish scholar, Mordecai Paldiel, summarizes his description of a *hasid* in a way that for a Christian is extraordinarily reminiscent of Yeshua's kenotic love and reference to the two great commandments of love: "A *hasid* is, then, a person who practices *hesed* in his or her daily life—in our parlance, a higher ethic. This, according to Jacobs, implies a disposition combining an intensity of love for God and the human being—a complete devotion to the former and an unqualified benevolence to the later.... As the Talmud points out, it is fitting for those who practice *hesed* to seek out the poor (*Shabbat* 104a)."[28]

Geza Vermes likewise stresses Yeshua's *hesed* and theocentric qualities, which he interestingly contrasts will Paul's Christocentrism: "Jesus' *hasiduth,* his *theocentric* devoutness, has been overlaid by the ramifications of Paul's *christocentric* spirituality. His opinion of human nature, unlike that of Jesus, was deeply pessimistic."[29]

Thus, in teaching and living his life in fulfilling the Torah and beyond in kenotic love, in *hesed,* the *hasid,* proto-rabbi Yeshua indeed lived a special, extraordinary life, the like of which his followers never before, or since, had experienced, but in this he was quintessentially Jewish.

Vermes thus sees *Yeshua* not as a barrier but a bond between Christians and Jews—and all human beings:

> In this so-called post-Christian era, when Christ as a divine form seems to ever-increasing numbers not to correspond, either to the age's notion of reality, or to the exigencies of the contemporary human predicament, is it not possible that Jesus the healer, teacher and helper may yet be invited to emerge from the shadows of his long exile? And not by Christians alone? If, above all, his lesson of reciprocal, loving and direct relation with the Father in heaven is recalled and found universally valid, may not the

sons of God on earth stand a better chance of ensuring that the ideal of human brotherhood becomes something more than a pipe-dream?[30]

## 2. The Pharisee-like Yeshua?

For nearly two thousand years most Christians have thought that Pharisaism, and subsequent Judaism said to have descended from it, were the enemy *par excellence* of Yeshua, and Christianity. However, recent research, mostly Jewish but also Christian, is calling this notion into serious question. Christians have much to learn about themselves from it.

There has been a great deal of scholarly debate in recent years about just who and what the Pharisees were.[31] This scholarly search for the "true Pharisees" is being pursued with such intensity for largely two reasons: some Jews have understood the Pharisees to be the forerunners of the rabbis, and therefore an essential link in the development of post-70 C.E. Judaism—referred to somewhat tautologically as Rabbinic Judaism. Christians have also traditionally made this same link between Phariseeism and Rabbinic Judaism and have further linked Rabbinic Judaism with the highly negative picture of the Pharisees portrayed in the gospels as the polar opposites of Yeshua. Though the sorting out of the scholarly puzzle is by no means complete, much has already been accomplished, especially by way of clearly setting aside a number of distortions. Hence, bearing in mind the incompleteness and at times the tentativeness of present-day scholarship as well as its advances, let us proceed to look briefly at the emerging image(s) of the Pharisees and Yeshua's relationship to them.

One of the most penetrating scholars in the area of Pharisaism is the Jew Ellis Rivkin.[32] He argues that the fundamental teaching not only of the post-70 rabbis but also of the Pharisees is a triad: "(1) The singular Father God so loved the individual that he (2) revealed, through Moses, his twofold Law which, if internalized and steadfastly adhered to, (3) would gain for such an individual eternal life for his soul and the resurrection of his body."[33] The second part of the triad, the twofold Law, is made up of the written Law, or Torah, i.e., the Scriptures, and the oral Torah, i.e., the rabbinic commentary and application of the written Torah.

A Christian scholar, John Pawlikowski, following the traditional path of linking closely the post-70 rabbis with the pre-70 Pharisees, but attributing the documented positive characteristics of the rabbis to the Pharisees as well, has written that through the use of the oral Torah process the Pharisees "deepened, humanized and universalized" the previous traditions. Whereas the priests focussed on the codification of the cultic legislation, the Pharisees, he states, concentrated on the "codification" of love, loyalty and human compassion, making them incumbent upon all the people Israel; general propositions were now spelled out as specific religious and moral duties to be lived out by all Jews. "Hospitality to travelers, visiting the sick of all religious groups, dowering the indigent bride, universal education for all males, attending the dead to the grave and helping to bring peace to those for whom it was absent" had never been clearly religious obligations in the Hebrew Scriptures, though they were implied in its spirit. "The rabbis fashioned these concerns into new commandments, or 'mitzvot.'"[34]

Often Christians have depicted Yeshua's intimacy with God his Father, or his insistence on the interior spirit of prayer and morality, as something new and opposed to the way of the Pharisees. Rivkin's research leads him to argue that the opposite is true. He finds that the source of the attractive power of the Pharisees was the relationship they established between the one God and the singular individual: "The Father God cared about *you;* He was concerned about *you.* He watched over *you;* He loved *you;* and loved *you* so much that He wished *your* unique self to live forever." For the Pharisees "The Heavenly Father was ever present. One could talk to Him, plead with Him, cry out to Him, pray to Him—person to Person, individual to Individual, heart to Heart, soul to Soul. It was the establishment of this personal relationship, an inner experience, that accounts for the manifest power of Pharisaism to live on.... *Internalization* is the only road to salvation."[35] Pawlikowski wrote in similar fashion that with the Pharisees "a sense of a new intimacy between God and the human peson was beginning to dawn. He had now become the Father of each and every person."[36]

The picture of the Pharisees that emerges from this research is that they were a group of lay scholar-teachers[37] who first appeared in history about a century and a half before the birth of Yeshua, developed the above teachings and practices, used proof-texting from the Bible as a technique, and became authoritative in the life of the Jews during the reign of Queen Alexandra (76-67 B.C.E.) long before Yeshua's day. This clearly was a revolution, for Moses gave no authority over the Torah and the religious life to any lay scholar class; nor indeed did the Bible use proof-texting as a technique—that was a peculiarly Pharisaic-rabbinic development. After the death of Queen Alexandra the influence of the Pharisees appeared to retreat, though by no means disappear. After the 70 C.E. destruction of Jerusalem they emerged as evidently influential in the areas around the Christian churches for which Mark and Matthew wrote (the use of the term Pharisee in Luke and John requires further careful examination), so that the quality of their importance in Matthew's milieu in particular (c. 85 C.E.) will be at least partly reflective of that period rather than solely of the time of Yeshua.  Bearing this differentiation in mind, it is clear that the New Testament offers irrefutable proof of the first century C.E. influence of the Pharisees:  In Matthew, chapter 23, which excoriates the Pharisees violently, Yeshua is nevertheless recorded to have said:  "The scribes and Pharisees sit on Moses' seat; so practice and observe whatever they tell you" (Mt. 23:2f.).  In Mt 5:20 Yeshua says: "Unless your righteousness *exceeds* that of the scribes and Pharisees, you will never enter the kingdom of heaven" (Mt. 5:20).  The context of this latter statement has Yeshua saying that he came to carry out the Torah (15:17), that it indeed will be completely carried out (15:18), that to teach the violation of the Torah is bad, its vindication good (15:19).  Therefore, the Pharisaic reverence for the Torah is to be emulated—and surpassed—by his followers (15:20).

This image of the Pharisees sounds dramatically the opposite of what Christians have had projected for themselves.  In fact, it appears extraordinarily like the image of Yeshua, and later that of his followers.  Rivkin noticed the same thing, for after speaking of the Pharisaic triad he described Yeshua as being nurtured on the twofold Torah: "The grand faith of the Pharisees in the Triad was inscribed within his conscience. God was indeed the loving and caring Father.  God had revealed...the twofold Law ...promised that everyone who served with love and loyalty would enjoy eternal life and resurrection.  For Jesus, as for the Pharisees, the ultimate reality was within, not without."[38]

As mentioned, it is argued by Rivkin that the custom of biblical proof-texting—including that of Christians—was originally a Pharisaic technique;[39] it is found only in the early (Pharisaic-)rabbinic (*tannaitic*) materials of the Mishnah, Tosefta,[40] etc., *not* in the Hebrew Bible, nor even in the apocryphal or pseudepigraphical writings.  However, Rivkin continues, these "Pharisaic" forms underlie the gospels, the Acts of the Apostles and the epistles of Paul.  Paul, for example, constantly cited Scripture in the "Pharisaic" manner.  When he wished to prove that God had made a covenant with Abraham before Abraham was circumcized, he clinched his argument with a conclusive proof text from Scriptures (cf. Rom. 4:1-12).  Yeshua refuted the Sadducees with a proof text (Mk. 12:12-27), and justified the expulsion of the money changers from the Temple with a proof text (Mk. 11:17-18).  "Indeed, wherever one turns within the gospels, one is offered proof text after proof text—a vivid testimony to how utterly normative this Pharisaic original had become."[41]

The authoritative position and attitude of the Pharisees that emerges from this line of thought is stunningly like that which numberless Christian scholars have claimed exclusively for Yeshua: Moses never granted a scholar class any authority over God's Law. Such authority had been given to prophets and priests, but not scholars. Yet nowhere in the Mishnah—recall that Rivkin maintains the traditional link between the rabbis and the Pharisees—is the *halakhah* expounded by either a prophetic or a priestly class. No *halakhah* is ever introduced with the prophetic formula "Thus says the Lord." Neither do we find in the Mishnah the priesthood as a class exercising any authority that is not on sufferance of the scholar class. Further, the Mishnah is the repository exclusively of the teachings of a scholar class. Because these teachings are presented as authoritative and binding, and because they are teachings which, for the most part, are not written down in the Pentateuch, "they testify to a system of *authority that is self-assumed, self-asserted, and self-validated*"[42] Hence, when Yeshua said things like "You have heard it said, but I say to you..." he was simply treading the (Pharisaic) rabbinic path. Indeed, Phillip Sigal has given abundant references to similar rabbinic usage, e.g., as noted above: "The form with which Jesus presents his strongest halakhic remarks, 'I say unto you,' (Mt. 5:22, 25, 32, 34, 39, 44) should not be regarded as evidence of anything more than proto-rabbinic insistence upon one's own view even when it contradicts and abolishes earlier teaching.... It is self-evident that people 'marvelled' at Menahem b. Sungai (*T. Ed.* 3:1) as they did at Jesus (Mt. 7:28)."[43]

A careful review of the ministry of Yeshua reveals many parallels between him and the proto-rabbinic (Pharisaic) movement: Yeshua is often seen in the process of teaching his oral Torah, reinterpreting the Hebrew Scriptures in a manner in line with the social setting in which he found himself. His emphasis on teaching falls into the general pattern of the authentic rabbi. Although Yeshua himself gave no clear indication of the type of institutional arrangements he wished his disciples to make after his death, the example of the early Jerusalem and Galilean churches, which can be presumed to reflect his teachings in at least a general way, shows great similarities to the synagogue model advocated by the proto-rabbis (Pharisees). Yeshua also participated in Pharisaic-type fellowship meals, instituting the Christian Eucharist at the final one he attended. "In the area of doctrine the resemblance continues: Emphasis on love, on the *Shema* [monotheism prayer], on the themes summarized in the Beatitudes and on the Resurrection indicate the presence of a strong Pharisaic spirit in the life of Jesus. In particular Jesus' stress on his intimate link with the Father picks up on a central feature of Pharisaic thought."[44]

Hence, it is not at all surprising that Pawlikowski, a Catholic, concluded that it would not be wrong "to consider Jesus as a part of the general

Pharisaic movement, even though in many areas he held a distinctive view-point."[45] The Protestant scholar E. P. Sanders is somewhat more cautious, but nevertheless moves in the same direction when he states, "I am one of a growing number of scholars who doubt that there were any substantial points of opposition between Jesus and the Pharisees."[46] The Jewish scholar Geza Vermes remarks, "not that there appears to have been any fundamental disagreement between Jesus and the Pharisees on any basic issue.... the conflict between Jesus of Galilee and the Pharisees of his time would, in normal circumstances, merely have resembled the in-fighting of factions belonging to the same religious body."[47]

It is likewise extremely important in terms of influencing preaching and teaching in the Catholic Church, and indirectly other Christian churches as well, that practically all of the above described research and reasoning on the Pharisees, including the positive as well as the negative relationship between them and Yeshua (and Paul as well), has been adopted by the Vatican Commission for Religious Relations with the Jews in its June 24, 1985 "Notes on the Correct Way to Present the Jews and Judaism in Preaching and Catechism in the Roman Catholic Church," as found in paragraphs 16-19, e.g., "It may also be stressed that, if Jesus shows him-self severe towards the Pharisees, it is because he is closer to them than to other contemporary Jewish groups."

Rabbi Harvey Falk has recently painstakingly argued for a nuancing of the claim of Yeshua's closeness to the Pharisees, stating that Yeshua stood with a particular school or "house" of Pharisees, the House of Hillel (*Bet Hillel*), rather than their opponents *Bet Shammai*.[48] It has long been gener-ally held by Christian scholars that in a number of disputes between Yeshua and Pharisees or Sadducees Yeshua defends the Pharisaic position of *Bet Hillel*. It has also been briefly alluded to by some Christian scholars "that it was Pharisaism, and that of the Shammaite kind, that dominated first-century Judaism,"[49] that "it was perhaps only after the fall of Jer-usalem that the Hillelites gained the ascendency."[50] Despite a rather un-critical handling of New Testament materials, Falk thoroughly analyzes the rabbinic materials (though he unfortunately does not deal critically with the dating problems) and argues that *Bet Shammai* was dominant in Judaism from about 30 B.C.E. to 70 C.E. (among other causes might be the fact that Hillel died around 10 C.E. but Shammai only around 30 C. E.), "and that the murderous Zealots, often represented in the priesthood in Jerusa-lem, were followers of Bet Shammai.... [and] demonstrate that the Sham-maites were responsible for handing Jesus over to the Romans for the cru-cifixion, and that their decision was in violation of Jewish law."[51] Falk further claims that the various criticisms of and attacks on the Pharisees by

Jesus are in fact attacks specifically on the narrow-minded Phariseeism of *Bet Shammai,* that Jesus was trying to bring Judaism back to the generous-hearted Phariseeism of *Bet Hillel,* who taught his followers to be "one who loves peace, pursues peace, loves mankind, and draws them [gentiles] nigh to the Torah."[52]

*Bet Hillel,* for example, taught that gentiles who live righteously—observe the Noahide commandments—will merit a share in the World to Come; *Bet Shammai* taught that they would not[53]—perhaps the so-called Judaizers that Paul opposed in Acts 15, and were described by Luke in unnuanced fashion as "Pharisees" (Acts 15:5), were of *Bet Shammai:* "But some men came down from Judea and were teaching the brethren, 'Unless you are circumcised according to the custom of Moses, you cannot be saved'" (Acts 15:1). Since after 70 C.E. subsequent Judaism rejected *Bet Shammai* in favor of *Bet Hillel,* the conclusion is drawn that, as

> The Talmud states explicitly, a Jew who follows the teachings of Bet Shammai "deserves death." Hence, there is no basis for Christian enmity toward the Jews of today because of the actions of certain individuals who lived in the first century. We do not identify with them nor with their teachings. A Heavenly Voice settled the matter toward the close of the first century: "The Halakhah is as Bet Hillel [teaches]."[54]

The latest and perhaps most insightful and even exciting research on this matter is the 1986 book by the Jewish scholar Rabbi Phillip Sigal from Pittsburgh—unfortunately a posthumous work. Sigal shows extraordinary scholarly expertise in both New Testament and rabbinic and other Jewish materials.

He argues that the Pharisees of the gospels are *not* the predecessors of the post-70 rabbis, from whom come the rabbinic writings and who are the clear "founders" of present-day Rabbinic Judaism. Rather, the Greek term *pharisaioi,* from the Hebrew *perushim,* meant largely what it said literally, "the separatists": "The *pharisaioi* in controversy with Jesus in Matthew are *perushim,* pietistic sectarian Jews of various circles whose identity is still not clear to us.... who were rigid in their halakhah, 'strict constructionists' in their hermeneutics and exegesis, and were therefore at serious odds with Jesus."[55] Sigal calls the predecessors of the rabbis—who came into existence as a clear group after the destruction of Jerusalem in 70 C.E. gathered around Yohanan ben Zakkai in the Palestinian village of Yavneh—"proto-rabbis." In Matthew's Gospel "the term *nomikos* [expert in the law] refers to a proto-rabbi. As over against a Sadducee, he too may be taken as a *parush* in colloquial idiom,"[56] but in reality he is quite distinct from the *perushim.*

Falk argues that the Pharisee opponents of Yeshua in the gospels were in fact Shammaites—who were basically repudiated by the post-70 rabbis, followers of Hillel (to whom Yeshua was *similar*)—and therefore, not the forerunners of present-day Rabbinic Judaism. Sigal makes a somewhat similar move, but argues that the pre-70 predecessors of the rabbis were neither Hillelites nor Shammaites, belonging to no school or "house" (*bet*) as such. Further, because he sees the proto-rabbis as operating much more as individuals in their interpretation of the rules of conduct, the *halakhah,* than the various pre-70 schools and groups, he can claim on the basis of his evidence and argument that Yeshua is not merely *like* or *near* the proto-rabbis. Rather, "he acted on principles that were not acceptable to *perushim* but were either already part of or destined to become part of proto-rabbinic and rabbinic Judaism. He was therefore an early proto-rabbi of the tannaitic era and taught halakhah accordingly. He was neither a Sadducee nor a Pharisee, neither a Hillelite nor a Shammaite. He employed freedom of interpretation and authority in conformity with the fashion of proto-rabbinic Judaism."[57]

As mentioned above, Sigal even makes a personal link between Yeshua and the post-70 rabbis of Yavneh by claiming that the founder of Yavneh and "rabbinism," Yohanan ben Zakkai, was not only a contemporary of Yeshua, but since he spent twenty years in Galilee, including before and during the time of Yeshua's public ministry, probably was a colleague of Yeshua:

> Jesus was first a disciple and then a colleague of proto-rabbis in Galilee. The most celebrated of those was Yohanan b. Zakkai. My conjecture is that Jesus and Yohanan were the same age and ultimately were colleagues in Galilee. Jesus would have been a mature disciple and colleague of proto-rabbis during the decade 20-30 when Yohanan b. Zakkai was in Galilee and Jesus was in his formative period. Both probably studied at both the schools of Hillel and Shammai and both took independent directions.... During Yohanan's period of leadership at Yavneh, no action was taken against Christians.[58]

The deaths of Hillel and Shammai are placed around the year 10 C.E. and 30 C.E., respectively, and the birth of Yeshua around 4 B.C.E. If these dates are reasonably accurate, it is even possible that Yeshua sat at the feet of either Hillel or Shammai themselves or both, especially when one recalls that Jewish lads came of age religiously and otherwise at the age of twelve. That Yeshua was already steeped in religious learning by that age is recorded in Luke 2: 40-52, where it is said that Yeshua was filled with wisdom and that he spent three days with the rabbis (*didaskalon*, "teachers," which is the term Luke uses here, is of course what *rabbi* means and is doubtless the Greek translation for *rabbi* used throughout the gospels in general) discussing religious matters with them and astonishing them with his answers. In any case, Yeshua obviously studied with the rabbis during his youth in Galilee, as did also Yohanan ben Zakkai. It would appear almost impossible that two such brilliant rabbinic students living and working in the same confined area of Galilee would not have learned of each other's teachings. Further, it does indeed seem quite likely that they would have sought each other out for extended discussion, as Sigal suggests. Of this, of course, we have no documentary proof, and so we are left with likelihood.

Sigal sees the reason for the expulsion of the followers of Rabbi Yeshua from Judaism not as being Yeshua's, or his followers' attitude toward the Law, or even because of theology in the early decades: "At no time during the first five decades after the crucifixion were Christian Judaism and pre-rabbinic Judaism wholly incompatible." But rather, "Post-70 Jews were antagonistic to the returned Christians at Jerusalem [they were "peace-people," like Yohanan ben Zakkai, who also fled the Roman war in the capital] and to the expansion and success of their movement [e.g., Saul's persecution of the followers of Yeshua, Acts 8:3]."[59] Whatever the reason for the antagonism, Sigal finishes his book with the following pregnant conclusion: "Had Christian Jews not been expelled from the synagogues after 90 A.D., but remained a segment of Judaism, it is well within the realm of possibility that Jesus would have secured a place in the proto-rabbinic pantheon."[60]

## 3. Yeshua, a Galilean Hasid?

At this point note should also be taken of the assertion by the Jewish scholar Geza Vermes that "the person of Jesus is to be seen as part of first-century charismatic Judaism and as the paramount example of the early Hasidim or Devout."[61] His argumentation is detailed and documented. Let an earlier description of the Hasidim by another scholar, Shmuel Safrai, suffice to illustrate the extraordinary parallels between them and Yeshua:

> Prominent in their doctrine is the importance attributed to good deeds in public life (redemption of captives, the digging of cisterns for the benefit of wayfarers, the restoration of lost property,

the consolation of mourners, the giving of alms etc.).... The Hasidim trust in God and sublime providence, are confident that it is not the snake but the sin that is fatal, and behave accordingly in actual practice, in full faith in God *even in cases in which such behavior opposes the accepted ruling.* Their confidence in providence and in the salvation resulting from right behavior, and even in the miracles which were to be revealed to them, stands in the numerous anecdotes told of Honi the Circlemaker, R. Hanina ben Dosa, Phineas ben Ya'ir and other Hasidim. They appeal to God as if commanding Him to make rain fall [conversely with Yeshua: calming of the storm, Mk. 4:49].... Among all the austerities practised by the Hasidim there is no trace of austerity in *halakhoth* concerning ritual purity, a subject which burst all bounds in Judaism. In effect, the only tradition which concerns subjects of purity accuses them of failing on a clearly explained passage of the Pentateuch which in itself is one of the principal sources for rulings on purity [Yeshua too was often accused of violating purity laws.][62]

What then of the relationship of these Hasidim—including Yeshua, if indeed, as it appears, he can be called one of them—to the Pharisees? Safrai has an interesting speculation which places the hasidim eventually within—albeit somewhat uneasily—the society of the Pharisees and rabbis (remembering that according to the gospels Yeshua was addressed as "rabbi") who developed their own literary traditions and interpretations of the Law (*halakhah*)—as did Yeshua: "As to the use of the concept 'Hasid'...as time went on, and perhaps as early as the end of the Hasmonaean period [63 B.C.E.], this concept became confined to a certain defined group within the society of the Pharisees and rabbis; this group had a literary tradition and its own halakhic practices."[63]

In reenforcement of Vermes' position, Phillip Sigal speaks of Yeshua not only as a proto-rabbi, but also as a charismatic, hasid-like figure: Yeshua was a *hakham* [a sage, a term Sigal identifies with proto-rabbi], a proto-rabbi, who has become spiritually converted and transformed into a charismatic prophet-figure. Like a prophet he preached fearlessly of awesome things, but like the *hakham* he taught halakhah along with his agadic preaching. In this function he employed the freedom of interpretation, the independent authority and methodology that was the style of proto-rabbinism.[64]

Thus perhaps the best way to see Yeshua within the context of the Judaism of his time is as a wandering, wonder-working teacher (*rabbi*), a sage (*hakham*), from Galilee, a Galilean *hasid,* who in many ways was similar to Hillel (whose teaching eventually came to prevail generally over Shammai's in Rabbinic Judaism), and whom some scholars would also see as having had a close relationship to the Pharisees centered in Jerusalem— whom he nevertheless criticized and who in turn criticized him. Sigal would see him as a Galilean *hasid,* a *hakham* and a proto-rabbi, who, like Yohanan ben Zakkai both before and after 70 severely criticized the *pharisaioi,* the *perushim* (whom Sigal does not identify as the predecessors of Rabbinic Judaism, even though at times a loose use of the term *pharisaioi* by the gospels and Josephus might include some proto-rabbis). I am persuaded that Sigal provides the most accurate and comprehensive description of Yeshua's place in the Jewish life of his time.

## 4. Development and Reinterpretation in the Bible

I feel compelled to say a few words here about the continuation of an ancient misstep that was first prominently exemplified by a second-century Christian, Marcion. It has been frequently restated anew, and most recently so by a fellow Catholic writer—who otherwise has been extraordinarily insightful and liberating—Franz Alt. The misstep I am talking about is the attempt to drive a wedge between the Hebrew Scriptures and the Apostolic Scriptures (in the past referred to by Christians as the Old and New Testaments).

I have no worry about Dr. Alt for he obviously is insightful, experienced, sensitive and more than capable of learning new ways of seeing things. (In this matter it would seem that he has been inappropriately influenced by the vitriolic anti-Judaism Dr. Hanna Wolff, who is creative as a psychologist but destructive as a Scripture scholar.) However, because Dr. Alt's book, *Jesus - der erste neue Mann,*[65] which has become so extraordinarily popular, having sold many scores of thousands of copies—and justifiably so—is so full of anti-Jewish statements that I feel compelled to offer, in addition to what I have already written above, what I believe are some minimal correctives to this very serious, corrosive mistake.

Let me first cite a few of the most problematic statements by Dr. Alt so the reader of this book will have some idea of the intensity of the anti-Jewish spirit permeating his widely-read, otherwise excellent book. Dr. Alt asserts that ancient Marcionite radical break between the "Old" Testament and the "New," especially contrasting the alleged understanding of God in the "Old" with that in the "New":

> "Aus dem strengen Richtergott des Alten Testaments war ein liebender Vater geworden" (p. 49).

"Nie war mir [Franz Alt] die Unvereinbarkeit des alttestamentlichen Richter-Gottes und des Liebas-Gottes Jesu so klar vor
Augen gestanden" (p. 118).

"Jede Harmonisierung und Vermischung des Gottesbildes Jesu
mit dem patriarchalischen Richter-Gottesbild des Alten Testaments ist Gift für lebendige Religion" (p. 118).

"Dieses ganz neue Gottesbild hat mit dem vorherrschend militan-
ten alttestamentlichen Gott nichts mehr zu tun" (p. 121).

"Hundertfach ist im Neuen Testament belegt, daß Jeschua das
Alte Testament nicht nur in Frage gestellt hat, sondern es über-
winden wollte" (p. 122).

"Jeschua hat nicht die Fortsetzung des Alten gemeint, auch nicht
die Harmonisierung mit dem Alten Testament" (p. 157).

In several places Alt even explicitly attempts to deny Yeshua's Jewishness:

"Den Patriarchen-Gott Jahwe, den die Juden kannten, nahm Jesus
gar nicht in den Mund" (p. 122). [In fact, from long before then
not only did Yeshua not utter the proper name of God, Yahweh,
but neither did *any* devout Jew, as anyone visiting a Jewish service would also experience today in their liturgical reading of the
Bible.]

"Jesus vertritt ein dynamische Gottesbild im Gegensatz zum sta-
tischen Gottesbild des orthodoxen Judentums" (p. 127).

"Mit dieser neuen ganzheitlichen Spiritualität hatte der Jude Jesus
aufgehört, Jude zu sein" (p. 131).

Franz Alt, of course, is unfortunately not the only contemporary author
to slip back into this traditional Christian triumphalism over the "Old" Testament. Many others continue to do so, as for example, Hildegunde
Wöller, as when among other similar remarks she says: "Die Kluft, die in
der alttestamentlichen Epoche aufgerissen worden ist, erst durch Jesus, den
Christus, überwunden wurde." And again: "Johannes des Täufers Rede at-
met den Zorngeist alttestamentlicher Propheten. Sein Gott ist ein eif-
ersüchtiger, rächender und strafender Gott wie Jahwe . . ."[66]

The major misunderstanding underlying this hostile contrasting of the
understanding of God in the Hebrew Scriptures with that of the New Testament is the mistaken assumption that the Hebrew Bible is a consistent,
unified whole. It is not. It is many different kinds of literature written over
many centuries. Nor does the New Testament present a single theological
view, even though in contrast to the Hebrew Bible it was written within

the span of a single lifetime—50 C.E. to 125 C.E. In the Hebrew Bible and other Jewish writings up to the time of Yeshua and shortly thereafter (it must be borne in mind that the New Testament is also a Jewish book, written mostly by, for and about Jews) there is a very significant evolution in the understanding of God and the appropriate human relationship to God and each other (ethics). Theodor Jaeckel makes this point clear in the subtitle of his book *Wer sich stören läßt, lebt. Die Entwicklung des Gottesverständnisses in der Bibel.* Of the early Hebrew conception of God he says: "Dieses Gottesverständnis war aber nicht starr; es konnte sich im Lauf der Zeit entwickeln."[67]

This clear fact is also ignored in the polemical contrasting of "the" Old Testament notion of God of justice with Yeshua's God of love. For example, although there is not always a steady upward evolution, one can see that in very ancient times the principle of "an eye for an eye" already was an advance over the endless family blood feuds that were prevalent (and still exist in some cultures), and that this principle was later replaced by the custom of substituting "financial" payment for physical punishment.

Or again, one can see the clear shift from the earlier image of a God commanding the smashing of the enemy baby against the rock to the image of God in the Book of Jonah who spares the repentant pagan city Niniveh—much to the disgust of Jonah. Eventually, as I detailed above, in the century or so before the time of Yeshua, one finds Jewish teachings which are full of urgings of loving one's neighbor and the depiction of God as a Father who loves each individual soul.

Moreover, one must be careful not to make parallel comparisons between the Hebrew Bible on the one hand and the teaching of Yeshua on the other. The former is a running account of the history and thought of a whole people over many centuries, whereas the latter is an articulation of the teaching and life of one person. If a comparison is to be made, the more correct one would be between the Hebrew Bible and the whole of the New Testament.

In the New Testament, just as in the "Old," there is no unified picture of God and the appropriate relationship of humans to God and each other (ethics). For example, the attitude in the New Testament towards women varies drastically: Yeshua has a very positive, feminist attitude; Paul of the accepted authentic epistles is moderate to negative (depending on whether 1 Cor. 14:34-36 is thought to be a non-Pauline interpolation or not); the deutero-Pauline writers and the author of 2 Peter are strongly anti-woman. Thus, the New Testament attitude toward women evolves—downward.

Something similar in the way of a negative evolution also happens in the New Testament attitude toward Yeshua's co-religionists, his fellow

Jews, like Mary, Joseph, Peter, James, John . . .—all his followers. It is clear that Yeshua's attitude toward his own people is one of loving concern. It seeps through all the Gospels, despite the varying hostility of the Gospel redactors, traditionally known as Mark, Luke, Matthew and John.

Yeshua's attitude toward his fellow Jews is clearly positive: "Salvation is from the Jews" (Jn 4:22). But then antipathy toward the perceived "founders" of Rabbinic Judaism, the Pharisees, moved in, distorting Yeshua's position, which was one of great similarity plus criticism and debate with particular groups among them—rabbis have always, to this very day, encouraged vigorous discussion and debate over the correct understanding of the Scriptures. The best known expert in the sociology of the New Testament, Gerd Theißen, has some very insightful remarks in this regard:

> Die Evangelien vermitteln heir ein einseitiges Bild. Sie sind in einer Zeit geschrieben (ca. 70-110 n. Chr.), in der aus der inner-jüdischen Eneuerungsbewqegung um Jesus eine Religion neben dem Judentum geworden war, die mit ihrer Mutterreligion konkurrierte. Ihre Schriften bieten oft nur ein verzerrtes Bild vom Judentum. Dem Bibelleser wird daher nicht klar, wie tief Jesus im Judentum verwurzelt ist.[68]

Beyond the attitude of Yeshua toward his fellow Jews in general and the Pharisees is the shift to that of the redactor of the Gospel of Mark, who is moderately critical of the Pharisees; then to Luke and Matthew, who are increasingly vituperative; and finally to John, the latest of the Gospels, where even the term for the "representatives" of Rabbinic Judaism, the Pharisees, is largely dropped in favor of the naked term, "the Jews," "*hoi judaioi.*" "The Jews" is repeated by John in machine-gun-like fashion seventy-two times!—with a killing effect in subsequent Christian history when the Passion of John was (is) read at the Good Friday liturgy. One result was that for centuries Jews were told not to go out during Holy Week, lest pogroms—having been incited by John's Gospel—be unleashed.

To be sure, Yeshua reinterpreted the Hebrew Bible in his own way, but far from making him no longer Jewish, this action of his made him pre-eminently Jewish. The story of the development of the Hebrew Bible is the story of the constant reinterpretation of the previous portions of the Bible. The so-called apocrypha (e.g., Ecclesiasticus, Maccabees, Wisdom, called deutero-canonical books by Catholics and Orthodox Christians) continued this Jewish practice, as did also the "intertestamental" Jewish writings, like the "Book of Jubilees" and "The Testaments of the Twelve Patriarchs."

And then so did Hillel and Shammai—and Yeshua and Johanan ben Zakkai and the subsequent Rabbis and Church Fathers down to present-day Jewish and Christian thinkers. In this reinterpretation of the Bible Yeshua, and his followers, understood themselves acting in a traditional Jewish manner—as indeed they were. In no way did he "cease being Jewish," as Dr. Alt maintained.

To tear Yeshua out of his Hebrew/Jewish heritage is to fundamentally distort his message—as I have argued all along. Making a radical break between the Hebrew Bible and the New Testament is the first fateful step in that direction, which leads to rootless confusion and an identity-crisis for Christians and a latent anti-Judaism, which, as we know from history, bears within it the seeds of antisemitism and the horrific possibility—become a reality—of the "Holocaust."

Franz Alt himself states the correct attitude concerning the right understanding of the relationship of the Hebrew Bible and the New Testament, between Judaism and Yeshua: "Nach Jesus ist das Einfache echt, nicht das Zwiespältige. Das ist echt Jesus. Wer es fühlt, weiß es (p. 125).

## 5. Implications for Christians

In sum, then, what does the Jewishness of Rabbi Yeshua mean to Gentile Christians? It means many things, of which we have briefly dwelled on only a few.

First, all of the false dichotomies outlined above, law and grace, justice and love, faith and works, with the denigration of one half, run absolutely counter to the teaching and life of Rabbi Yeshua. Such polarizations must be rejected by anyone who claims to be a follower of Rabbi Yeshua, of Jesus.

Secondly, Rabbi Yeshua clearly affirmed the keeping of the entire Torah as he interpreted it, for himself and his Jewish followers.

Thirdly, recalling from the previous chapter, Rabbi Yeshua was not the *Meshiach* promised to the Jews; rather, he became the *Christos* of the gentiles, through whom gentiles came to know the one true God and through whom they became part of the one people Israel.

Fourthly, also from the previous chapter, Rabbi Yeshua and his first followers thought and spoke within the Jewish framework of meaning, and consequently the only way for Christians to understand his gospel is to understand it Jewishly—including the Jewish non-ontological way of understanding Messiah, Son of God, etc.

Fifthly, one of the immediate implications of the research, on Yeshua and the Pharisees is that Yeshua, far from being in intense opposition to the forerunners of the Yavneh rabbis and subsequent Rabbinic Judaism, was very like them, close to them, one of them, perhaps even a colleague in his youth of the founder of Rabbinic Judaism, Yohanan ben Zakkai. Rather than seeing Yeshua as breaking away from Judaism, as Christians from an early period have been wont to do, they should be inclined to link him closely with the Judaism of his day. They should see him as an important, indeed, along with Yohanan ben Zakkai, a pioneering, figure in the development of Judaism in continuity with its biblical past and rabbinic future. Remembrance of this link was apparently broken by the way his disciples proclaimed him and definitively by post-90 historical developments. In light of this research, then, Christians will need to rethink their relationship with Judaism in the founding period of Christianity, and subsequently.

Sixthly, it is that last point, the subsequent Christian relationship to Judaism, however, that is the most painful to reflect on. Nevertheless, we Christians must study the history and present reality of our relations with Yeshua's co-religionists, the Jews. We Christians have had a two-thousand-year history of suspicion, denigration, oppression, hatred, robbery, rapine, murder and genocide of Jews. The horrible paradox is that we Christians claim to be the followers of Rabbi Yeshua, who was a Jew. We claim he shows us how to live a human life, and therefore we try to imitate him. We speak of *Imitatio Christi*. But when we hate Jews we hate what Yeshua was, a Jew. We hate then what we say we are trying to be, a kind of Jew, one who has been led to the one true God, the God of Abraham, Isaac, Jacob, Sarah, Rachel and Rebecca through Rabbi Yeshua the Christ. We hate the people Israel, that "good olive tree onto which we wild shoots have been grafted" (Rom. 11: 17-24).

Thus, the Christian must reject Antisemitism not only on general humanitarian grounds, but also because it is a hatred of God's Chosen People (and Paul reminds us that God never goes back on God's promises); we must reject Antisemitism because it is a hatred of the Jew Yeshua, whom we call Lord and say we love and imitate; and thus, lastly, we must reject Antisemitism because it is self-hatred. Instead of being Antisemites, we Christians should be philosemites, for Yeshua, Jesus, was a Jew, and we are followers of Rabbi Yeshua and members of his people.

# Notes

1. Pinchas Lapide and Hans Küng, "Is Jesus a Bond or Barrier? A Jewish-Christian Dialogue," *Journal of Ecumenical Studies*, 14 (1977), p. 473, a translation of, Hans Küng und Pinchas Lapide, *Jesus im Widerstreit. Ein jüdisch-christlicher Dialog* (Stuttgart/Munich: Calwer-Kösel, 1976, p. 26.

2. Franz Mussner, *Traktat über die Juden* (Munich: Kösel, 1979); English translation, *Tractate on the Jews*, by Leonard Swidler (Philadelphia: Fortress, 1984), p. 118.

3. David Flusser, *Jesus in Selbstzeugnissen und Bilddokumenten* (Reinbeck, 1968), p. 43.

4. Joseph Klausner, *Jesus of Nazareth* (New York, 1925), p. 275.

5. Nicolas de Lange, "Who Is Jesus?" *Sidic*, 12, 3 (1979), p. 12.

6. Johann Maier, "Jesus von Nazareth und sein Verhältnis zum Judentum aus der Sicht eines Judaisten," in Willehad Paul Eckert and Hans Hermann Henrix, eds., *Jesu Jude-Sein als Zugang zum Judentum*, 2nd ed. (Aachen: Einhard, 1980), p. 95.

7. Cf. Julius Wellhausen, *Einleitung in die drei ersten Evangelien*, (Berlin: Reimer, 1905), p. 113: "Jesus was not a Christian; he was a Jew."

8. E. P. Sanders, *Jesus and Judaism* (Philadelphia: Fortress, 1985), p. 264.

9. A word has many possible meanings; the one intended can be known only in relation to its context, as was in this case again pointed out by Gerhard Delling: "The meaning of *pleroo* cannot be deduced...it must be based on the context.... According to Mt. 5:17a this [mission of Yeshua] is primarily fulfillment of the Law and prophets.... Jesus does not merely affirm that He will maintain them. As He sees it, His task is to actualise the will of God made known in the OT." Gerhard Kittel, *Theological Dictionary of the New Testament* (Grand Rapids, MI: Eerdmans, 1968, VI, pp. 293ff. For a thorough discussion of the meaning of *plerosai* and the attitude of Yeshua toward the Law see Mussner, *Traktat über die Juden*, pp. 185-93; *Tractate on the Jews*, pp. 115-121.

10. Phillip Sigal, *The Halakhah of Jesus of Nazareth according to the Gospel of Matthew* (Lanham, MD: University Press of America, 1987), p. 18.

11. Geza Vermes, *Jesus and the World of Judaism* (Philadelphia: Fortress, 1983), p. 168.

12. I am especially indebted to Pinchas Lapide for this understanding of Matthew's treatment of the attitude of Yeshua toward the Law (Torah) and his supererogatory ideal; conversation in Frankfurt, July 8, 1985.

13. E. P. Sanders, *Jesus and Judaism*, pp. 330; 263ff.

14. Mussner, *Tractate on the Jews*, p. 121.

15. Sigal, *The Halakhah of Jesus*, p. 6.

16. Ibid., p. 16.

17. *Mishnah*, Sotah, 9,9.

18. Sigal, *The Halakhah of Jesus*, p. 159.

19. Ibid., pp. 81f.

20. Ibid., p. 79.

21. Vermes, *Jesus and the World of Judaism*, p. 68.

22. Ibid. Geza Vermes noted on the one hand that, "Jesus...more than once expressly urges obedience to the purely ritual and cultic precepts in sayings all the more historically credible in that they are peripheral to the gospel narrative and actually run counter to the essential antinomianism of Gentile Christianity."

    But he adds that, "the chief distinction of Jesus' piety lies in his extraordinary emphasis on the real inner religious significance of the commandments.... Philo and Josephus did the same. So did many of the rabbis, and the Qumran sectaries.... Interiority, purity of intention, played a greater part in Jesus' thought...because of his natural bias towards the individual and personal rather than the collective." *Jesus and the World of Judaism*, p. 47.

23. Ibid., p. 55.
24. Louis Jacobs, "The Concept of Hasid in the Biblical and Rabbinic Literature," *Journal of Jewish Studies*, vol. 8 (1957), p. 150.
25. Cf. e.g., *Yalkut Shimone*, Erev, 873, and *Sifri*, Erev, 49.
26. Mordcai Paldiel, "*Hesed* and the Holocaust," *Journal of Ecumenical Studies*, 23, 1 (Winter, 1986), p. 95.
27. *Talmud*, Avodah Zarah, 20b.
28. Paldiel, "*Hesed* and the Holocaust," p. 97.
29. Vermes, *Jesus and the World of Judaism*, p. 56.
30. Ibid., p. 57.
31. See Louis Finkelstein, *The Pharisees*, 2 Vols. (Philadelphia: Jewish Publication Society, 1962); R. Travers Herford, *The Aim and Method of Pharisaism*, republished as *The Pharisees* (Boston: Beacon Press, 1962); Asher Finkel, *The Pharisees and the Teacher of Nazareth* (Leiden: Brill, 1964); Jacob Neusner, *The Rabbinic Traditions about the Pharisees before 70*, 3 vols. (Leiden: Brill, 1971); John Bowker, *Jesus and the Pharisees* (London: Cambridge University Press, 1973). For updating articles see: Michael Cook, "Jesus and the Pharisees. The Problem as It Stands Today," *Journal of Ecumenical Studies*, 15,3 (Summer, 1978), pp. 441-460; Leonard Swidler, "The Pharisees in Recent Catholic Writing," *Horizons*, 10,2 (Fall, 1983), pp. 267-287; Lewis Eron, "Implications of Recent Research on the Pharisees for Jewish-Christian Dialogue," in Leonard Swidler, ed. *"Breaking Down the Wall" between Americans and East Germans, Jews and Christians—Through Dialogue* (Lanham, MD: University Press of America, 1987), pp. 131-160.
32. Ellis Rivkin, *A Hidden Revolution* (Nashville, TN: Abingdon, 1978). Rivkin's method is to analyze separately the three bodies of early literature that deal with the Pharisees: The New Testament, late first century C.E.; the Jewish historian Josephus, late first century C.E.; early rabbinic writings, e.g., Mishnah, codified late second century, but including materials going back to 200 B.C.E. He concludes that they all come out with fundamentally the same image of the Pharisees.

Until recently almost all Christian scholars have been simply ignorant of rabbinic literature. Even now many are reluctant to admit its helpfulness in understanding the New Testament. Christians have often been so bent on insisting on Yeshua's difference from his contemporary fellow Jews that they discount the validity of Mishnaic materials when they produce rabbinic parallels to teachings or actions of Yeshua. It is true that much work remains to be done on the form-critical analysis and dating of these rabbinic writings (Jacob Neusner and his students have been hard at work on the task for years). Nevertheless, if the Mishnah, or even the two Talmuds (codified at the end of the fourth and fifth centuries respectively), attribute a teaching to a predecessor or contemporary of Yeshua, the logical assumption should be to accept its accuracy until some counter evidence challenges it. Such rabbinic documentation would not, of course, be the strongest possible documentary evidence, for the later redactors of the Mishnah and Talmuds reshaped the cited material for their contemporary purposes. It would be stronger, however, than the simple *a priori* assumption that it is not valid merely because it appears in a later codified document. The burden of proof is on the "rejectionist" Christian scholar, not the one who carefully uses rabbinic documents.

A Christian scholar of the targumic literature, Martin McNamara, who has made a study of its relevance to the New Testament, not only says much the same but goes further:

We are still left with the delicate task of how to approach rabbinic material for New Testament studies. Authors, as already noted, differ on the point and most probably will continue to do so. A legitimate, and probably wise, approach would appear to be the following: accept rabbinic tradition as the continuation of the Pharisaic tradition of New Testament times and earlier, and regard both as being in the same spirit. Even if a given formulation of rabbinic tradition may be later, it is to be presumed as being in the spirit of earlier Pharisaism. We may freely have recourse to the rabbinic tradition for New Testament studies because of this. Since later development in the rabbinic tradition cannot be denied, however, care must be taken to ascertain the date of each rabbinic tradition used in New Testament studies.... The problem of dating will always remain with us in the use of this material, and the efforts being made to refine our methodology in its use must continue. But the problems in assigning an exact date to individual pieces of rabbinic tradition are amply offset by the realization that the tradition as a whole has every appearance of continuing the form of Judaism with which Christ and his followers had the closest contact. *Palestinian Judaism and the New Testament* (Wilmington: Michael Glazier, 1984), pp. 177, 204.

The Jewish scholar Geza Vermes, as an expert in both the Jewish literature and the New Testament, categorically supports this position: "Rabbinic literature skilfully handled, is still the richest source for the interpretation of the original gospel message, and the most precious aid to the quest for the historical Jesus." *Jesus and the World of Judaism*, p. 125.

33. Rivkin, *A Hidden Revolution*, p. 293.

34. John T. Pawlikowski, *Christ in the Light of the Christian-Jewish Dialogue* (New York: Paulist Press, 1982), p. 82.

35. Rivkin, *A Hidden Revolution*, p. 310. The Christian scholar Joachim Jeremias in a number of places has argued that Yeshua's addressing God as *Abba,* Father, was unique and indicated an extraordinarily intimate relationship between Yeshua and God. However, as Rivkin argues, to address God as Father was already something traditionally Pharisaic. Of course God was referred to as Father in the older Hebrew Bible numerous times. In addition, God is addressed as Our Father, *Abinu,* in Jewish, i.e., Pharisaic-Rabbinic, prayers, carefully traced back to the years 10-40 C.E. by Louis Finkelstein, *Phariseeism in the Making.* New York: KTAV, 1972, pp. 259f. There is also evidence that the ancient hasidim—devout Jews living in Palestine before the birth of Yeshua—"spent an hour (in recollection before praying) in order to direct their hearts towards their Father in heaven," from the *Mishnah,* Ber. 5:1. There is even evidence that precisely the child's term of endearment for father, *Abba,* was used by the first-century Palestinian Jew Hanan to refer to God in prayer: "When the world was in need for rain, the rabbis used to send school-children to him, who seized the train of his cloak and said to him, *Abba, Abba,* give us rain! He said to God: Lord of the universe, render a service to those who cannot distinguish between the *Abba* who gives rain and the *Abba* who does not." *Bab. Talmud* Ta'an 23b. Since here the structure of the whole story is formed around the fact that *Hanan* referred to God in prayer with the same term for father (*Abba*) used by the children to address him, Hanan, the use of the term *Abba* could not be a retrojection into the story from the time of the codification of the Talmud. And *Hanan* was a grandson of Honi the Circle-maker, who we know was an adult before Jerusalem fell to Pompey in 63 B.C.E. (See Geza Vermes, *Jesus the Jew.* Philadelphia: Fortress Press, 1973, pp. 72, 210f.) So, the events of this story probably occurred some years before the birth of Yeshua.

Vermes added to the arguments against Jeremias' *"Abba"* claim in a later book:

Jeremias understood Jesus to have addressed God as "Dad" or "Daddy," but apart from the *a priori* improbability and incongruousness of the theory, there seems to be no linguistic support for it. Young children speaking Aramaic addressed their parents as *abba* or *imma* but it was not the only context in which *abba* would be employed. By the time of Jesus, the determined form of the noun, *abba* (= "the father"), signified also "my father"; "*my* father," though still attested in Qumran and biblical Aramaic, had largely disappeared as an idiom from the Galilean dialect. Again, *abba* could be used in solemn, far from childish, situations such as the fictional altercation between the patriarchs Judah and Joseph reported in the Palestinian Targum, when the furious Judah threatens the governor of Egypt (his unrecognized brother) saying: "I swear by the life of the head of *abba* (= my father) as you swear by the life of the head of Pharaoh, your master, that if I draw my sword from the scabbard, I will not return it there until the land of Egypt is filled with the slain," *Jesus and the World of Judaism* (Philadelphia: Fortress Press, 1983), p. 42).

Although Georg Schelbert in "Sprachgeschichtliches zu 'abba'," Pierre Casetti, et al., eds., *Melanges Dominique Barthelemy*. Orbis Biblicus et Orientalis, 38 (Fribourg: Editions Universitaires Fribourg, 1981), pp. 395-447 confirms that "the word play with 'abba' certainly belongs to the original form of the tradition" of the gospel story being analyzed, he argues that it is not possible to be certain that the text as we have it is *verbatim* from before the time of Jesus. Nevertheless, as a result of his most thoroughgoing analysis of all the pertinent Aramaic texts and inscriptions, he concludes that, "In the Aramaic language of the time of Jesus, there was absolutely no other word [than *Abba*] available if Jesus wished to speak of or address God as father. Naturally such speaking of and addressing thereby would lose its special character, for it is then indeed the only possible form!" (p. 396). He notes that Jeremias' claim of "special character" for the use by Yeshua—and world-wide popularization of that claim—was not only unwarranted but that this error was also recognized by others (e.g., such recognized scholars as H. Conzelmann, D. Flusser, E. Käsemann, E. Hänchen), and later even partly by Jeremias himself, although "the consequences were really not drawn in his text," nor were the contradictory opinions of the other scholars "hardly really taken account of" (p. 396). Moreover, Schelbert shows in great detail that the Mishnah "without any doubt manifests an extremely intimate relationship to God as 'Father in heaven'" (p. 419).

36. Pawlikowski, *Christ in the Light*, p. 88.

37. Jacob Neusner in his three-volume work *The Rabbinic Traditions about the Pharisees Before 70* argues that the Pharisees were essentially *haberim*, a small pacifist party concerned with purity. Rivkin rejects this, as does also E. P. Sanders: "His [Neusner's] analysis of the Rabbinic texts is unpersuasive and is made especially dubious by the evidence from Josephus." E. P. Sanders, *Jesus and Judaism*, p. 188.

38. Rivkin, *A Hidden Revolution*, p. 303.

39. Rivkin finds the rabbis in the rabbinic writings, all of which were codified after the writing of the gospels, using the proof-texting method. Because he sees the Pharisees as the predecessors of the rabbis, he attributes this practice to them. However, the only first-century "Jewish" document other than the New Testament (wherein Yeshua and Paul do indeed proof-text) which evidences the practice of proof-texting are the Dead Sea schools of the Qumranites. So perhaps it would be safer to say that the technique of proof-texting was widely practiced in pre-70 Judaism, which of course included the Pharisees, but not claim that the Pharisees invented the practice.

40. "Mishnah" means teaching which is recited orally (as does also the Arabic term "Qur'an"), coming from "shani," "to repeat." The Aramaic root "teni" has the same meaning, and therefore the teachers of this material are known as "tannaim." The "Tosefta" is a collection of halakhic teaching omitted from the 200 C.E. edition of the Mishinah and edited probably shortly afterwards; the term means "supplement." The Palestinian Talmud (the term means "instruction"), by far the shorter of the two Talmuds, was edited around the year 400 C.E., the Babylonian Talmud around 500 C.E. The Talmud consists of quotations of the Mishnah and commentary known as "Gemara," coming from the root "gamar," "to complete." The rabbis responsible for the "Gemara" are known as "amoraim," meaning "interpreters."

41. Rivkin, *A Hidden Revolution*, pp. 273f.

42. Ibid., p. 232; italics added.

43. Phillip Sigal, *The Halakhah of Jesus*, pp. 81f.

44. Pawlikowski, *Christ in the Light*, pp. 92f.

45. Ibid., p. 92.

46. Sanders, *Jesus*, p. 264.

47. Vermes. *Jesus and the World of Judaism*, p. 11.

48. Harvey Falk, *Jesus the Pharisee* (New York: Paulist Press, 1985).

49. W. D. Davies, *Paul and Rabbinic Judaism* (London: SPCK, 1970), p. 54.

50. George Foot Moore, *Judaism in the First Centuries of the Christian Era* (Cambridge: Harvard University Press, 1927), vol. 1, p. 81.

51. Falk, *Jesus the Pharisee*, pp. 8f.

52. *Mishnah*, Avot 1:12.

53. Cf. Gerd Theissen, *Sociology of Early Palestinian Christianity* (Philadelphia: Fortress Press, 1977), p. 83: "The result was that in the first century AD they [the Pharisees] split into two schools.... Thus the Shammaites required strict separation from the Gentiles. In eighteen halachoth, there were prohibitions against various Gentile foods, the Greek language, Gentile testimony, Gentile gifts, sons and daughters-in-law (j.Shab.3c 49ff.). They even used force against the Hillelites to carry through these intensified norms (j.Shab.3c 34ff.). Only after the catastrophe of AD 70 did the more moderate Hillelites succeed in gaining the upper hand."

54. Falk, *Jesus the Pharisee*, p. 158.

55. Sigal, *Halakhah of Jesus*, pp. 9, 4.

56. Ibid., p. 163.

57. Ibid., p. 9.

58. Ibid., pp. 248ff.

59. Ibid., pp. 7f.

60. Ibid., p. 159.

61. Vermes, *Jesus the Jew*, p. 79.

62. S. Safrai, "Teaching of Pietists in Mishnaic Literature," *The Journal of Jewish Studies*, XVI, 1-2 (1965), pp. 32f.

63. Ibid., pp. 33.

64. Sigal, *The Halakhah of Jesus*, p. 154.

65. Franz Alt, *Jesus - der erst neue Mann* (Munich: Piper Verlag, 1990)—5 printing, 150,000 copies.

66. Hildegunde Wöller, *Ein Traum von Christus. In der Seele geborn, im Geist erkannt* (Stuttgart: Kreuz Verlag, 1987), pp. 70-71.

67. Theodor Jaeckel, *Wer sich stören läßt, lebt. Die Entwicklung des Gottesverständnisses in der Bibel* (Stuttgart: Quell Verlag, 1988), p. 15.

68. Gerd Theißen, *Der Schatten des Galiläers. Historicshe Jesusforschung in erzählender Form* (Munich: Chr. Kaiser Verlag, 1989—8 printing, 45,000 copies), p. 20.

CHAPTER 3

# Yeshua, Feminist and Androgynous: an Integrated Human

In a certain sense the whole of human life is a complex series of encounters on a variety of levels and in manifold directions: the encounter of the human being with its own self, with nature around it, with its fellow human beings and with ultimate reality—in the Judeo-Christian tradition called God. This complex of encounters redound on and influence each other: whoever leaves the encounter of the human with ultimate reality aside, for example, will distort the human relationship to itself, to nature and to fellow humanity. Only in the present day are we becoming fully aware that the encounter with our environment and nature is rapidly transforming the world into a place where humans can no longer meet each other in a human manner; indeed, we may soon no longer be able to exist at all if we do not succeed in reversing the pollution of our environment.

History is the story of the encounters of humans with themselves and their fellow humans—and it is too infrequently a joyful account. Often humans appear to flee from an encounter with their true selves and appear all too seldom really to encounter their fellow humans; far too often they meet them as objects, but do not encounter them as persons. That, however, means that they do not meet them as they really are. Still worse is the long history of the dehumanizing of humans by one another, a dehumanizing in various ways and in various degrees. Fortunately one of the crassest forms of the "exploitation of man by man," slavery, has been largely eliminated. Even the elimination of economic slavery has made significant progress in recent centuries—although the remaining task in this area is staggeringly great.

However, even the complete elimination of economic exploitation in the customary sense would still leave half of the human race in conditions which systematically distort and degrade their humanity. Which half of the human race? The female half. Women are thought almost by nature to be submissive, subordinate, second-class—not as slaves in the usual sense, but rather as something humanly even more unworthy: voluntarily submissive, willing slaves. They are often trained, programmed so that they are eager to be only half-humans, and specifically the "passive" half. Of course, as in every master-slave relationship, the humanness of the master is distorted as well as that of the slave. Men too are often trained, programmed to be half-humans, the "aggressive" half.

It is no solution, as one is wont to suggest, that the sexes naturally mutually complete each other so that a human whole is formed when the two half-humans are united, as for example, in marriage. Even our colloquial speech tells us that this notion is false. To be "passive" is not normally thought of as virtuous, any more than being "aggressive" is. In the relationship of one human being to another the passivity of one does not complement the aggressiveness of the other, but abets it. To be sure, all human beings must combine receptivity and assertiveness, softness and firmness, feeling and clear thinking. However, this combination must be present in *every* person. Every woman and every man must be receiving as well as giving, soft and firm, emotional and rational, in order to be a complete human. However, the structures of almost all societies tend to split the human person into two halves, the male and female, and even to insist that this is prescribed in natural law. Biology is transformed into ontology! But in fact women are no more constituted primarily by their sex than are men; they are primarily human, *persons*—just as men are.

Christians are not distinguished from other people in that they are or try to be anti-human, un-human or super-human. As all other people, Christians strive to be complete in their humanity, but they believe that they have found in Yeshua the model of full humanity. Yeshua is the Christians' model of the encounter with God, nature, with one's self, one's fellow human beings, especially the oppressed, that is, the physically sick, the poor, the ignorant—and women. For centuries Christians have attempted to imitate Yeshua in all these encounters, except the last named one. And yet, the encounter between man and woman is the most basic, pervasive of all the exploitative encounters in the history of humanity. It is the encounter which most pressingly needs the liberating model of Yeshua. Perhaps because it is the most fundamental, final bastion of sinful humanity, that is, of egocentric unfree humanity, that it is the last to yield to the liberating grace in Yeshua.

Put in one word, the model that Yeshua provided, the burden of everything that he thought, taught and wrought, was "liberation." According to Luke 4:18 he quoted Isaiah of himself: "He has sent me to bring the good news to the poor, and to proclaim *liberty*," and according to John 8:32, 36 he said, "If you make my word your home...you will learn the truth and the truth will make you *free*.... If the son makes you *free*, you will be *free* indeed." Fundamentally this liberation is a freeing from ignorance and hence from a bondage to a false self and a false perception of reality, that is, first of all of our fellow human beings, then all things around us, and through them the Source of all reality. Then the human being is free to reach out in love to her/his own true self, fellow humans, nature and the Source of all.

If indeed the most exploitative encounter between human beings is the encounter of men with women, and hence is most in need of Yeshua's liberating model, so too is the encounter with the self in a similar need in a very closely related manner. As the Jungian psychologist Hanna Wolff put it: "Jesus is the first male who broke through the androcentricism of antiquity. The despotism of the solely male values is deposed. Jesus is the first one who broke with the solidarity of men, that is, of non-integrated men, and their anti-feminine animus. Jesus stands before us as the first man without animus."[1] The so-called feminine and masculine characteristics were exemplified in Yeshua in integrated, liberating—"androgynous"—fashion, and he presented a similar mutual, liberating model in the encounter with nature and with God. It is on the first two of those encounters—men with women, and with self—that we will focus through the model Yeshua presented.

## A. Yeshua Was a Feminist

Perhaps today is the *kairos* when this most basic rampart of oppression will finally yield to the power of the combination of the model of Yeshua and the grace of the moment, the contemporary secular movement toward a full, equal human development of women: feminism. What is the model of Yeshua's encounter with women? If we look at the gospels not with the eyes of male chauvinism or the eternal feminine, we will see that the model Yeshua presents is that of a feminist: Yeshua was a feminist. A feminist is a person who is in favor of, and who promotes, the equality of women with men, a person who advocates and practices treating women primarily as human persons (as men are so treated) and willingly contravenes social customs in so acting.

To prove the thesis it must be demonstrated that, so far as we can tell, Yeshua neither said nor did anything which would indicate that he advocated treating women as intrinsically inferior to men, but that on the contrary he said and did things which indicated that he thought of women as the equals of men, and that in the process he willingly violated pertinent social mores.

The negative portion of the argument can be documented quite simply by reading through the four gospels. Nowhere does Yeshua treat women as "inferior beings." In fact, it is apparent that Yeshua understood himself to be especially sent to the typical classes of "inferior beings" such as the poor, the lame, the sinner—and women—to call them all to the freedom and equality of the reign of God. But there are two factors which raise this negative result exponentially in its significance: the status of women in Palestine at the time of Yeshua, and the nature of the gospels. Both need to be recalled here in some detail, particularly the former.

## 1. The Status of Women in Palestine

The status of women in Palestine during the time of Yeshua was very decidedly that of inferiors. Despite the fact that there were several heroines recorded in the Hebrew Scriptures, according to most rabbinic customs[2] of Yeshua's time—and long after—women were not allowed to study the Scriptures (Torah). One first century rabbi, Eliezer, put the point sharply: "Rather should the words of the Torah be burned than entrusted to a woman.... Whoever teaches his daughter the Torah is like one who teaches her lasciviousness."[3]

In the vitally religious area of prayer, women were so little thought of as not to be given obligations of the same seriousness as men. For example, women, along with children and slaves, were not obliged to recite the *Shema,* the morning prayer, nor prayers at meals.[4] In fact, the Talmud states: "Let a curse come upon the man who (must needs have) his wife or children say grace for him."[5] Moreover, in the daily prayers there was a threefold thanksgiving: "Praised be God that he has not created me a gentile; praised be God that he has not created me a woman; praised be God that he has not created me an ignorant man."[6] (It was obviously a version of this rabbinic prayer that Paul controverted in his letter to the Galatians: "There is neither Jew nor Greek, there is neither slave nor free, there is neither male nor female; for you are all one in Christ Jesus," Gal. 3:28.) Women were also greatly restricted in public prayer. It was not even possible for them to be counted toward the number necessary for a quorum to form a congregation to worship communally (a *minyan*)[7]—they were again classified with children and slaves, who similarly did not qualify (there is an interesting parallel to the canon 93 of the 1917 Roman Catholic *Codex Juris Canonici,* CIC—valid until 1983—which grouped married women, minors, and the insane). In the great temple at Jerusalem they were limited to one outer portion, the women's court, which was five steps below the court for the men.[8] In the synagogues the women were also separated from the men, and of course were not allowed to read aloud or take any leading function.[9] (The same is still true in many Orthodox synagogues today—canon 1262 of the 1917 CIC also stated that "in church the women should be separated from the men.")

Besides the disabilities women suffered in the areas of prayer and worship there were many others in the private and public forums of society. The "Proverbs of the Fathers" contain the injunction: "'Speak not much with a woman.' Since a man's own wife is meant there, how much more does not this apply to the wife of another? The wise men say: 'Who speaks much with a woman draws down misfortune on himself, neglects the words of the law, and finally earns hell.'"[10] If it were merely the too free intercourse of the sexes which was being warned against, this might signify nothing derogatory to woman. But since a man may not speak even to his own wife, daughter or sister in the street,[11] then only male superiority can be the motive, for intercourse with uneducated company is warned against in exactly the same terms: "One is not so much as to greet a woman."[12] In addition, save in the rarest instances, women were not allowed to bear witness in a court of law.[13] Some Jewish thinkers, as for example, Philo, a contemporary of Yeshua, thought women ought not leave their households except to go to the synagogue (and that only at a time when most of the other people would be at home);[14] girls ought even not cross the threshold that separated the male and female apartments of the household.[15]

In general, the attitude toward women was epitomized in the institutions and customs surrounding marriage. For the most part the function of women was thought of rather exclusively in terms of childbearing and rearing; women were almost always under the tutelage of a man, either the father or husband, or if a widow, the dead husband's brother. Polygamy—in the sense of having several wives, but *not* in the sense of having several husbands—was legal among Jews at the time of Yeshua, although probably not heavily practiced. Moreover, divorce of a wife was very easily obtained by the husband—he merely had to give her a writ of divorce; women in Palestine, on the other hand, were not allowed to divorce their husbands.

Rabbinic sayings about women also provide an insight into the attitude toward women: "It is well for those whose children are male, but ill for those whose children are female."[16] "At the birth of a boy all are joyful, but at the birth of a girl all are sad."[17] "When a boy comes into the world, peace comes into the world: when a girl comes, nothing comes."[18] "Even the most virtuous of women is a witch."[19] "Our teachers have said: Four qualities are evident in women: They are greedy at their food, eager to gossip, lazy and jealous."[20]

Conclusion: The condition of women in Palestinian Judaism was that of inferiors.

## 2. The Nature of the Gospels

As noted earlier, the gospels are not the straight factual reports of eye witnesses of the events in the life of Yeshua of Nazareth as one might find in the columns of the *New York Times* or the pages of a critical biography. Rather, they are four different faith statements reflecting at least four primitive Christian communities who believed that Yeshua was the Messiah. They were composed from a variety of sources, written and oral, over a period of time and in response to certain needs felt in the communities and individuals at the time; consequently they are many-layered. Since the gospel writer-editors were not twentieth-century critical historians, they were not particularly intent on recording the very words of Yeshua, the *ipsissima verba Jesu*, nor were they concerned to winnow out all of their own cultural biases and assumptions. Indeed, it is doubtful that they were particularly conscious of them.

This modern critical understanding of the gospels, of course, does not impugn the historical character of the gospels; it merely describes the type of historical documents they are so their historical significance can more accurately be evaluated. Its religious value lies in the fact that modern Christians are thereby helped to know much more precisely what Yeshua meant by certain statements and actions as they are reported by the first Christian communities in the gospels. With this new knowledge of the nature of the gospels it is easier to make the vital distinction between the religious truth that is to be handed on and the time-conditioned categories and customs involved in expressing it.

## 3. Yeshua as Source

When the fact that no negative attitudes by Yeshua toward women are portrayed in the gospels is set side by side with the recently discerned "communal faith-statement" understanding of the nature of the gospels, the importance of the former is vastly enhanced. For whatever Yeshua said or did comes to us only through the lens of the first Christians. If there were no very special religious significance in a particular concept or custom we would expect that current concept or custom to be reflected by Yeshua. The fact that the overwhelmingly negative attitude toward women in Palestine did not come through the primitive Christian communal lens by itself underscores the clearly great religious importance Yeshua attached to his positive attitude—his feminist attitude—toward women: Feminism, that is, personalism extended to women, is a constitutive part of the Gospel, the Good News, of Yeshua.

It should also be noted here that although in the analysis that follows it is the image of Yeshua as it emerges from the four gospels that will be dealt with, the feminist character that is found there is ultimately to be attributed to Yeshua himself and not to the Church, the evangelists or their sources. Basically the "principle of dissimularity" operates here. That principle, devised by contemporary New Testament scholars, states that if a saying or action attributed to Yeshua is contrary to the cultural milieu of the time, then it most probably had its origin in Yeshua. In this case the feminism of Yeshua could hardly be attributable to the primitive Church.

As is seen already in the later New Testament writings, the early Church quickly became not only non-feminist, but also anti-woman. For example: "The women should keep silence in the churches. For they are not permitted to speak, but should be subordinate, as even the law says" (1 Cor. 14:34); "Let a woman learn in silence with all submissiveness. I permit no woman to teach or to have authority over men; she is to keep silent" (1 Tim. 2:11-12). The misogynist slide continued after the New Testament: In the second century Tertullian, the "father of theology," said of woman: "You are the devil's gateway";[21] in the next century Origen wrote: "What is seen with the eyes of the creator is masculine, and not feminine, for God does not stoop to look upon what is feminine and of the flesh";[22] in the fourth century Epiphanius said: "The devil seeks to vomit out his disorder through women."[23]

As seen in some detail before, in the Jewish culture women were held to be, as the first century Jewish historian Josephus put it, "in all things inferior to the man."[24] Since it was out of that milieu that the evangelists were writing and from which they drew their sources, neither of them could have been the source of the feminism found in the Yeshua of the gospels. Its only possible source was Yeshua himself. In fact, given the misogynist tendency exhibited both in the Judaism of Yeshua's time and in the early Christian Church, there is every likelihood that the strong feminism of Yeshua has been muted in the gospels, as can be seen for example by the fact that the story of the woman taken in adultery (Jn. 8:2-11) is absent from the earliest Greek manuscripts and almost did not make it into the canon of the New Testament at all.[25]

## 4. Yeshua as Jew

A further word of caution is needed here. The matter of Yeshua's relationship to Judaism and his attitude toward women is one that is fraught with difficulties. The first difficulty arises from the age-old Christian tendency to tear Yeshua out of his Jewish context. As already has been seen in some detail, for Christians, not only did everything Yeshua did *have* to be superlatively good, but whenever possible—and even where it was not legitimately possible—it also had to be *different* from things in Judaism. It was even better if it could be argued that it was opposed to the Jewish way of doing things.

In many ways Jewish scholars frequently reinforced this pattern of interpretation by either accepting a Christian (mis)reading of the gospels which interpreted Yeshua as un- or anti-Jewish, or (and) making Yeshua less than authentically Jewish by anachronistically making later talmudic Rabbinic Judaism the norm for pre-70 Judaism.

Fortunately these tendencies to dejudaize Yeshua and to retroject talmudic Judaism to the lifetime of Yeshua have begun to be counteracted in some recent Jewish and Christian scholarship. As has been noted, an increasing number of Jewish scholars are reclaiming Yeshua as an authentic Jew (German Jewish scholarship speaks of the "Heimholung Jesu") while an increasing number of the best-informed Christian scholars are persuaded that Yeshua can be properly understood only in his historical—Jewish—context, and agree that Yeshua was thoroughly Jewish.

Because at the same time Jewish, and Christian, scholarship is becoming ever more aware of the great variety of positions that were abroad within a very pluralistic pre-70 Judaism, it is becoming simultaneously aware that great caution needs to be employed in judging what was acceptably Jewish and what was not at that time.

This more pluralistic understanding of pre-70 Judaism also allows for greater differences among Jewish proponents of sometimes dramatically varying positions, without their being read out of Judaism *ex post facto*. These developments make it increasingly possible for Christians and Jews alike to both affirm Yeshua's Jewishness and at the same time grant that in some matters he differed from his contemporaries, just as many of them at times differed dramatically from each other.

The Jewish culture of the time of Yeshua indeed treated women as inferior to men, as did also much of the surrounding cultures, and Yeshua did in this matter run counter to that culture.[26] In the matter of Yeshua's attitude toward women, the evidence in the Gospels, however it is analyzed through form, redaction, source, audience, etc. criticism, points both negatively and positively toward a positive, personalist—and therefore, "feminist"—attitude by Yeshua toward women. From the documentation we have available, Yeshua stands out strongly in the Semitic cultural world in this regard, but not in total contrast to all before and around him.

In this matter of personalism extended especially to the marginalized of society, he stands centrally in the Jewish prophetic tradition and also within the pattern of the Galilean "wandering charismatics," some of whom seemed to have evidenced a more positive attitude toward women. Thus, concerning the place of women, though Yeshua does not seem to have distinguished himself from other Jews *qualitatively*, he certainly does *quantitatively*. We have nowhere near the amount of evidence of a personalist—feminist—attitude toward women (which is all the stronger for its indirect character) for other Jews as we do for Yeshua.

The problem arises when Christian feminist writers proceed unaware of the above developments in Jewish and Christian scholarship concerning early Judaism and Yeshua's place within it. They then tend to:

1) unnuancedly claim that our Yeshua had this wonderful attitude toward women and those Jews had a bad attitude?

2) write as though in this matter, as in allegedly so many others, Yeshua was un- or even anti-Jewish, having no precedents whatsoever for his position;

3) depict the lot of Jewish women at the time as even more of an inferior than a careful reading of the evidence would allow; and then, probably worst of all,

4) boast that *therefore* Christianity is superior to Judaism in its treatment of women—forgetting entirely that Yeshua was not a Christian, but a Jew, and that to the extent his personalist, feminist, attitude toward women was accepted, it took place *within* Judaism, whereas in "Christianity," as evidenced in the later New Testament writings (letters to Timothy, Second Peter, etc.), it was clearly rejected until the present day. In the case of women, as in that of other marginalized groups, Yeshua raised a powerful prophetic (and therefore, Jewish) voice of protest.

But it needs to be remembered that raising a prophetic voice was precisely a Jewish thing to do; in this Yeshua was not acting in a non-Jewish manner, but in a specifically Jewish tradition. Moreover, after the first enthusiastic response of the women followers to this liberating feminist move by Yeshua, the Christian Church quickly sank back into a non-feminist, even misogynist, morass until our time. There is no ground here for Christians to claim superiority over Jews, but rather just the opposite. Christians claim to be followers of Yeshua, whereas Jews do not. Christians therefore had far more reason to be, like Yeshua, feminists. But they—we—failed miserably.

## 5. Women Disciples of Yeshua

One of the first things noticed in the gospels about Yeshua's attitude toward women is that he taught them the Gospel, the meaning of the Scriptures, and religious truths in general. When it is recalled that in Judaism it was considered improper, and even "obscene," to teach women the Scriptures, this action of Yeshua was an extraordinary, deliberate decision to break with a custom invidious to women. Moreover, women became disciples of Yeshua not only in the sense of learning from him, but also in the sense of following him in his travels and ministering to him.[27] A number of women, married and unmarried, were regular followers of Yeshua. In Luke 8.1ff. several are mentioned by name in the same sentence with the Twelve: "He made his way through towns and villages preaching and proclaiming the Good News of the reign of God. With him went the Twelve as well as certain women.... who ministered to (*diekonoun*) them out of their own resources."[28] The significance of this phenomenon of women following Yeshua about, learning from and ministering to him, can be properly appreciated only when it is recalled that not only were women not to read or study the Scriptures, but in the more observant settings they were not even to leave their household, whether as a daughter, wife, or member of a harem.

## 6. Women and Resurrection from the Dead

Within this context of women being disciples and ministers, Yeshua quite deliberately broke another custom disadvantageous to women. According to the gospels Yeshua's first appearance after his resurrection to any of his followers was to a woman (or women), who was then commissioned by him to bear witness of the risen Yeshua to the Eleven (Jn. 20: 11ff.; Mt. 28:9f.; Mk. 16:9ff.). In typical male Palestinian style, the Eleven refused to believe the women since, according to Judaic law, women were not allowed to bear legal witness. Clearly this was a dramatic linking of a very definite rejection of the second-class status of women with a central element of the Gospel, the resurrection. The effort centrally to connect these two points is so obvious—an effort certainly not attributable to the male disciples or evangelists—that it is an overwhelming tribute to male intellectual myopia not to have discerned it effectively in two thousand years. In this case the source obviously was the women followers of Yeshua.

The intimate connection of women with resurrection from the dead is not limited in the gospels to that of Yeshua. There are accounts of three other resurrections in the gospels—all closely involving a woman. The most obvious connection of a woman with a resurrection acount is that of the raising of a woman, Jairus' daughter (Mt. 9:18ff.; Mk. 5:22ff.; Lk. 8:41ff.). A second resurrection Yeshua performed was that of the only son of the widow of Nain: "And when the Lord saw her, he had compassion on her and he said to her, 'Do not weep.'" (Cf. Lk. 7:11ff.) The third resurrection Yeshua performed was Lazarus', at the request of his sisters Martha and Mary (cf. Jn. 11). From the first it was Martha and Mary who sent for Yeshua because of Lazarus' illness. But when Yeshua finally came Lazarus was four days dead. Martha met Yeshua and pleaded for his resurrection: "Lord, if you had been there, my brother would not have died. And even now I know that whatever you ask from God, God will give you." Then followed Yeshua's raising of Lazarus from the dead. Thus, Yeshua raised one woman from the dead, and raised two other persons largely because of women.

There are two further details that should be noted in these three resurrection stories. The first is that only in the case of Jairus' daughter did Yeshua touch the corpse—which made him ritually unclean. In the cases of the two men Yeshua did not touch them, but merely said, "Young man, I say to you, arise," or, "Lazarus, come out." One must at least wonder why Yeshua chose to violate the laws for ritual purity in order to help a woman, but not a man. The second detail is in Yeshua's conversation with Martha after she pleaded for the resurrection of Lazarus. Yeshua declared himself to be the resurrection ("I am the resurrection and the life."), the only time he did so that is recorded in the gospels. Yeshua here again revealed a central element in the Gospel—the resurrection—to a woman.

## 7. Women as Sex Objects

There are of course numerous occasions recorded in the gospels where women are treated by various men as second-class citizens. There are also situations where women were treated by others not at all as persons but as sex objects, and it was expected that Yeshua would do the same. The expectations were disappointed. One such occasion occurred when Yeshua was invited to dinner at the house of a skeptical Pharisee (Lk. 7:36ff.) and a woman of ill repute entered and washed Yeshua's feet with her tears, wiped them with her hair and anointed them. The Pharisee saw her solely as an evil sexual creature: "The Pharisee...said to himself, 'If this man were a prophet, he would know who this woman is who is touching him and what a bad name she has.'" But Yeshua deliberately rejected this approach to the woman as a sex object. He rebuked the Pharisee and spoke solely of the woman's human, spiritual actions; he spoke of her love, her unlove, i.e., her sins, her being forgiven, and her faith. Yeshua then addressed her (it was not "proper" to speak to women in public, especially "improper" women) as a human person: "Your sins are forgiven.... Your faith has saved you; go in peace."

A similar situation occurred when the scribes and Pharisees used a woman reduced entirely to a sex object to set a legal trap for Yeshua (Jn. 8:2-11). It is difficult to imagine a more callous use of a human person than the "adulterous" woman was put to by the enemies of Yeshua. First, she was surprised in the intimate act of sexual intercourse (quite possibly a trap was set up ahead of time by the suspicious husband), and then dragged before the scribes and Pharisees, and then by them before an even larger crowd that Yeshua was instructing: "making her stand in full view of everybody." They told Yeshua that she had been caught in the very act of committing adultery and that Moses had commanded that such women be stoned to death (Dt. 22:22ff.). "What have you to say?" The trap was partly that if Yeshua said Yes to the stoning he would be violating the Roman law, which restricted capital punishment, and if he said No, he would appear to contravene Mosaic law. It could also partly have been to place Yeshua's reputation for kindness toward, and championing the cause of, women in opposition to the law and the condemnation of sin. Yeshua of course eluded their snares by refusing to become entangled in legalisms and abstractions. Rather, he dealt with both the accusers and the accused directly as spiritual, ethical, human persons. He spoke directly to the accusers in the context of their own personal ethical conduct: "If there is one of you who has not sinned, let him be the first to throw a stone at her." To the accused woman he likewise spoke directly with compassion, but without approving her conduct: "'Woman, where are they? Has no one condemned you?' She said, 'No one, Lord.' And Yeshua said, 'Neither do I condemn you; go, and do not sin again.'"

(One detail of this encounter provides the basis for a short excursus related to the status of women. The Pharisees stated that the woman had been caught in the act of adultery and according to the Law of Moses was therefore to be stoned to death. Since the type of execution mentioned was stoning, the woman must have been a "virgin betrothed," as referred to in Dt. 22:23f. There provision is made for the stoning of *both* the man and the woman, although in the gospel story only the woman is brought forward. However, the reason given for why the man ought to be stoned was not because he had violated the woman, or God's law, but: "because he had violated the wife of his neighbor." It was the injury of the man through the misuse of his property—wife—that was the great evil.)

## 8. Yeshua's Rejection of the Blood Taboo

All three of the synoptic gospels insert into the middle of the account of raising Jairus' daughter from the dead the story of the curing of the woman who had an issue of blood for twelve years (Mt. 9:20ff.; Mk. 5:25ff.; Lk. 8:43ff.). What is especially touching about this story is that the affected woman was so reluctant to project herself into public attention that she "said to herself, 'If I only touch his garment, I shall be made well.'" Her shyness was not because she came from the poor, lower classes, for Mark pointed out that over the twelve years she had been to many physicians—with no success—on whom she had spent all her money. It was probably because for twelve years, as a woman with a flow of blood, she was constantly unclean (Lv. 15:19ff.), which not only made her incapable of participating in any cultic action and made her in some sense "displeasing to God," but also rendered anyone and anything she touched (or anyone who touched what she had touched!) similarly unclean. (Here was the basis for the Catholic Church's not allowing women in the sanctuary during Mass until after Vatican II—she might be menstruating, and hence unclean.) The sense of degradation and contagion that her "womanly weakness" worked upon her over the twelve years doubtlessly was oppressive in the extreme.

This would have been especially so when a religious teacher, a rabbi, was involved. But not only does Yeshua's power heal her, in one of his many acts of compassion on the downtrodden and afflicted, including women, but Yeshua also makes a great to-do about the event calling extraordinary attention to the publicity-shy woman: "And Yeshua, perceiving in himself that power had gone forth from him, immediately turned about in the crowd, and said, 'Who touched my garments?' And his disciples said to him, 'You see the crowd pressing around you, and yet you say, "Who touched me?" And he looked around to see who had done it. But the woman, knowing what had been done to her, came in fear and trembling and fell down before him and told him the whole truth. And he said to her, 'Daughter, your faith has made you well; go in peace, and be healed of your disease.'" It seems clear that Yeshua wanted to call attention to the fact that he did not shrink from the ritual uncleanness incurred by being touched by the "unclean" woman (on several occasions Yeshua rejected the notion of ritual uncleanness), and by immediate implication rejected the "uncleanness" of a woman who had a flow of blood, menstruous or continual. Yeshua apparently placed a greater importance on the dramatic making of this point, both to the afflicted woman herself and the crowd, than he did on avoiding the temporary psychological discomfort of the embarrassed woman, which in light of Yeshua's extraordinary concern to alleviate the pain of the afflicted, meant he placed a great weight on teaching this lesson about the dignity of women.

## 9. Yeshua and the Samaritan Woman

On another occasion Yeshua again deliberately violated the then common code concerning men's relationship to women. It is recorded in the story of the Samaritan woman at the well of Jacob (Jn. 4:5ff.). Yeshua was waiting at the well outside the village while his disciples were getting food. A Samaritan woman approached the well to draw water. Normally a Jew would not address a Samaritan, as the woman pointed out: "Jews, in fact, do not associate with Samaritans." But also normally a man would not speak to a woman in public (doubly so in the case of a rabbi). However, Yeshua startled the woman by initiating a conversation. The woman was aware that on both counts, her being a Samaritan and being a woman, Yeshua's action was out of the ordinary for she replied: "How is it that you, a Jew, ask a drink of me, a woman of Samaria?" As hated as the Samaritans were by the Jews, it is nevertheless clear that Yeshua's speaking with a woman was considered a much more flagrant breach of conduct than his speaking with a Samaritan, for John related: "His disciples returned, and were surprised to find him speaking to a *woman,* though none of them asked, 'What do you want from her?' or, 'Why are you talking to her?'" However, Yeshua's bridging of the gap of inequality between men and women continued further, for in the conversation with the woman according to John he revealed himself in a straightforward fashion as the Messiah for the first time: "The woman said to him, 'I know that Messiah is coming'.... Yeshua said to her, 'I who speak to you am he.'"

Just as when according to the gospel Yeshua revealed himself to Martha as "the resurrection," and to Mary as the "risen one" and bade her to bear witness to the apostles, Yeshua here also, according to John, revealed himself in one of his key roles, as Messiah, to a woman—who immediately bore witness of the fact to her fellow villagers. It is interesting to note that apparently the testimony of women carried greater weight among the Samaritans than among the Jews, for when the villagers came out to see Yeshua: "Many Samaritans of that town believed in him on the strength of the woman's testimony." It would seem that John the gospel writer deliberately highlighted this contrast in the way he wrote about this event, and also that he clearly wished to reinforce thereby Yeshua's stress on the equal dignity of women.

One other point should be noted in connection with this story. As the crowd of Samaritans was walking out to see Yeshua, Yeshua was speaking to his disciples about the fields being ready for the harvest and how he was sending them to reap what others had sown. He was clearly speaking of the souls of men and women, and most probably was referring directly to the approaching Samaritans. Such exegesis is standard. It is also rather standard to refer to "others" in general and only Yeshua in particular as having been the sowers whose harvest the apostles were about to reap (e.g., in the Jerusalem Bible). But it would seem that the evangelist also meant specifically to include the Samaritan woman among those sowers for immediately after he recorded Yeshua's statement to the disciples about their reaping what others had sown he added the above-mentioned verse: "Many Samaritans of that town had believed in him on the strength of the *woman's* testimony."

## 10. Marriage and the Dignity of Woman

One of the most important stands of Yeshua in relation to the dignity of women was his position on marriage. His unpopular attitude toward marriage (cf. Mt. 19:10: "The disciples said to him, 'If such is the case of a man with his wife, it is not expedient to marry.'") presupposed a feminist view of women; they had rights and responsibilities equal to men. It was quite possible in Jewish law for men to have more than one wife (though this was probably not frequently the case in Yeshua's time, there are recorded instances, e.g., Herod, Josephus), though the reverse was not possible. Divorce, of course, also was a simple matter, to be initiated only by the man. In both situations women were basically chattel to be collected or dismissed as the man was able and wished to; the double moral standard was flagrantly apparent. Yeshua rejected both by insisting on monogamy and the elimination of divorce; both the man and the woman were to have the same rights and responsibilities in their relationship toward each other (cf. Mk. 10:2ff.; Mt. 19:3ff.). This stance of Yeshua was one of the few that was rather thoroughly assimilated by the Christian Church (in fact, often in an over-rigid way concerning divorce, for here Yeshua was offering a goal ethic, not a minimum ethic—but, how to understand the ethical prescriptions of Yeshua is another subject), doubtless in part because it was reinforced by various sociological conditions and other historical accidents, such as the then current strength in the Greek world of the Stoic philosophy. However, the notion of equal rights and responsibilities was not extended very far within the Christian marriage. The general role of women was *Kirche, Kinder, Küche*—and only a suppliant's role in the first.

## 11. The Intellectual Life for Women

However, Yeshua clearly did not think of woman's role in such restricted terms, she was not to be limited to being *only* a housekeeper. Yeshua quite directly rejected the stereotype that the proper place of all women is "in the home" during a visit to the house of Martha and Mary (Lk. 10:38ff.). Martha took the typical woman's role: "Martha was distracted with much serving." Mary, however, took the supposedly "male" role: she "sat at the Lord's feet and listened to his teaching." (It should be noted that this is a technical term for being a disciple—which is even reflected in contemporary English speech when we say: I sat at the master's feet.) Martha apparently thought Mary was out of place in choosing the role of the "intellectual," for she complained to Yeshua. But Yeshua's response was a refusal to force all women into the stereotype; he treated Mary first of all as a person (whose highest faculty is the intellect, the spirit) who was allowed to set her own priorities, and in this instance had "chosen the better part." And Yeshua applauded her: "It is not to be taken from her." Again, when one recalls the Palestinian restriction on women studying the Scriptures or studying with rabbis, that is, engaging in the intellectual life or acquiring any "religious authority," it is difficult to imagine how Yeshua could possibly have been clearer in his insistence that women were called to the intellectual, the spiritual life just as were men.

There is at least one other instance recorded in the gospels when Yeshua uttered much the same message (Lk. 11:27f.). One day as Yeshua was preaching, a woman from the crowd apparently was very deeply impressed and, perhaps imagining how happy she would be to have such a son, raised her voice to pay Yeshua a compliment. She did so by referring to his mother, and did so in a way that was probably not untypical at that time and place. But her image of a woman was sexually reductionist in the extreme (one that largely persists to the present): female genitals and breasts. "Blessed is the womb that bore you, and the breasts that you sucked!" Although this was obviously meant as a compliment, and although it was even uttered by a woman, Yeshua clearly felt it necessary to reject this "baby-machine" image of women and insist again on the personhood, the intellectual and moral faculties, being primary for all: "But he said, 'Blessed rather are those who hear the word of God and keep it!'" Looking at this text it is difficult to see how the primary point could be anything substantially other than this. Luke and the tradition and Christian communities he depended on must also have been quite clear about the sexual significance of this event. Otherwise, why would he (and they) have kept and included such a small event from all the months, or even years, of Yeshua's public life? It was not retained *merely* because Yeshua said blessed are those who hear and keep God's word (for the evangelist had already recorded that elsewhere), but because that was stressed by Yeshua as being primary in comparison to a woman's sexuality. Luke, however, seems to have had a discernment here, and elsewhere, concerning what Yeshua was about in the question of women's status that has not been shared by subsequent Christians (nor apparently by many of *his* fellow Christians), for, in the explanation of this passage, Christians for two thousand years did not see its plain meaning—doubtless because of unconscious presuppositions about the status of women inculcated by their cultural milieu.

## 12. Women in Yeshua's Language

Yeshua's attitude toward women is also reflected in the very language attributed to him in the gospels. First, Yeshua often used women in his stories and sayings, something most unusual for his culture. Secondly, the images of women Yeshua used were never negative, but rather always positive—in dramatic contrast to his predecessors and contemporaries. Thirdly, these positive images of women were often very exalted, at times being associated with the "reign of heaven," likened to the chosen people, and even to God herself! Fourthly, Yeshua often taught a point by telling two similar stories or using two images, one of which featured a man and one a woman. This balance, among other things, indicated that Yeshua wanted it to be abundantly clear that his teaching, unlike that of other rabbis, was intended for both women and men—and he obviously wanted this to be clear to the men as well as the women, since he told these stories to all his disciples and at times even to crowds. These sexually parallel stories and images also confirm the presence of women among his hearers; they were used to bring home the point of a teaching in an image that was familiar to the women.

The sexually parallel stories and images used by Yeshua range from very brief pairings to lengthy parables. Their frequency in the synoptic gospels is impressive—nine of them. For example, the reign of heaven was likened to a mustard seed which a man sowed and to leaven which a woman put in her dough (Mt. 13:31-33; Lk. 18-21), or, in the final days one man of two in the field and one woman of two grinding corn will be taken (Mt.24: 39-41).[29] The ultimate in sexually parallel stories told by Yeshua, however, was the one in which God was cast in the likeness of a woman.

## 13. God as a Woman

Yeshua strove in many ways to communicate the notion of the equal dignity of women. In one sense that effort was capped by his parable of the woman who found the lost coin (Lk. 15:8ff.), for here Yeshua projected God in the image of a woman. Luke recorded that the despised tax-collectors and sinners were gathering around Yeshua, and consequently the Pharisees and scribes complained. Yeshua, therefore, related three parables in a row, all of which depicted God's being deeply concerned for that which was lost. The first story was of the shepherd who left the ninety-nine sheep to seek the one lost— the shepherd is God. The third parable is of the prodigal son—the father is God. The second story is of the woman who sought the lost coin—the woman is God! Yeshua did not shrink from the notion of God as feminine. In fact, it would appear that Luke's Yeshua included this womanly image of God quite deliberately at this point for the scribes and Pharisees were among those who most of all denigrated women—just as they did the "tax-collectors and sinners."

There have been some instances in Christian history when the Holy Spirit has been associated with a feminine character, as, for example, in the third-century Syrian *Didascalia* where, in speaking of various offices in the Church, it states: "The Deaconess however should be honored by you as the image of the Holy Spirit." It would make an interesting investigation to see if these images of God presented here by Luke were ever used in a Trinitarian manner—thereby giving the Holy Spirit a feminine image. A negative result to the investigation would be as significant as a positive one, for this passage would seem to be particularly apt for a later Christian Trinitarian interpretation: the prodigal son's father is God the Father (this interpretation has in fact been quite common in Christian history); since Yeshua elsewhere identified himself as the Good Shepherd, the shepherd seeking the lost sheep is Yeshua, the Son (this standard interpretation is reflected in, among other things, the often-seen picture of Yeshua carrying the lost sheep on his shoulders); the woman who sought the lost coin should "logically" be the Holy Spirit. If such an interpretation has existed, it surely has not been common. Should such lack of "logic" be attributed to the general cultural denigration of women, or the Christian abhorrence of pagan goddesses—although the Christian abhorrence of pagan male gods did not result in a Christian rejection of a male image of God?

**14. Conclusion**

From this evidence it should be clear that Yeshua vigorously promoted the dignity and equality of women in the midst of a very male-dominated society: Yeshua was a feminist, and a very radical one.

# B. An "Androgynous" Yeshua

There is, however, also another message about Yeshua's attitude toward women and men to be found in the psychological image of Yeshua that is projected by the gospels. That image is of an androgynous person, not in the sense of a combination of physical male and female characteristics, but rather the fusion and balance of so-called masculine and feminine psychological traits.

The notion that the significance of Yeshua lay in his humanity rather than specifically in his maleness is one that was stated clearly and even officially already in early Christianity. In the Nicene creed (325 A.D.) ancient Christians said of Yeshua, "et *homo* factus est," "and he became *human.*" They did *not* say, "et *vir* factus est," "and he became *male* [*virile*]." There was even a limited amount of Christian painting of Yeshua as physically androgynous, but it was not very fully developed. However, if the question is asked whether the image of Yeshua in the gospels reflects the psychologically so-called masculine or feminine traits, abundant material for an answer is at hand.

One of the humanly very destructive things our culture does is popularly to divide up various human traits into feminine and masculine ones, as if women naturally had one set and men the other. Such a division is scientifically unfounded; in fact scientific data is piling up which tend to indicate that such a division of traits as allegedly inborn is largely fallacious. Hence, even to continue to use the terms feminine characteristics and masculine characteristics tends to perpetuate the problem. So, until sexually neutral terms are developed and widely used, I will refer to these two sets of characteristics as *so-called* feminine and masculine characteristics.

Certain ways of acting, thinking, speaking, etc., then, are popularly said to be specifically manly and their opposites womanly. 1) Men are supposed to be reasonable and cool—women are to be persons of feeling and emotion; 2) men are to be firm, aggressive—women, gentle, peaceful; 3) men should be advocates of justice—women, mercy; 4) men should have pride and self-confidence—women should have humility and reserve; 5) men are said to be the providers of security (food, clothing, shelter)—women, the ones who need security; 6) men are supposed to be concerned with organization and structure—women with persons, especially children. Analyzing the gospel image of Yeshua, in which of these divisions did he fit?

## 1. Reasonable and Cool—Feeling and Emotion

Yeshua had a large number of vigorous, at times even extremely vicious, enemies, both in debate and in life and death situations. In debate: After Yeshua criticized the chief priests and scribes, "they waited their opportunity and sent agents to pose as men devoted to the Law to fasten on something he might say and so enable them to hand him over to the jurisdiction and authority of the governor. They put to him this question, 'Master, we know that you say and teach what is right; you favor no one, but teach the way of God in all honesty. Is it permissible for us to pay taxes to Caesar or not?'" They were a clever lot, for Israel was occupied by Roman troops and the Jews in general consequently hated everything Roman with a passion, and especially the publicans (native tax-collectors for Rome). If Yeshua said straight out to pay Roman taxes, he would have immediately lost his influence with the people, which would have suited his enemies. But if he said do not pay taxes, he would have immediately ended up in a Roman jail, or perhaps worse, which also would have suited his enemies.

"But he was aware of their cunning and said, 'Show me a denarius. Whose head and name are on it?' 'Caesar's,' they said. 'Well, then,' he said to them, 'give back to Caesar what belongs to Caesar—and to God what belongs to God.'" A most *reasonable* response: "As a result, they were unable to find fault with anything he had to say in public; his answer took them by surprise and they were silenced" (Lk. 20:20-26).

In life and death situations: "When they heard this everyone in the synagogue was enraged. They sprang to their feet and hustled him out of the town, and they took him up to the brow of the hill their town was built on, intending to throw him down the cliff." Yeshua's reaction? "But he slipped through the crowd and walked away" (Lk. 4:28-30). Real *cool.*

More examples could be given, but these would seem sufficient to place Yeshua in the "masculine" camp for category one.

On the other hand, once when Yeshua came to the little town of Nain he saw a funeral procession for a young man, "the only son of his mother, and she was a widow." The widow was in a desperate situation for in that culture women had almost no legal or economic standing except through a man—father, husband, son. Understandably the woman was weeping. A pitiable sight. But here Yeshua's reaction wasn't "cool." "When the Lord saw her he *felt* sorry for her. 'Do not cry' he said. Then he went up and put his hand on the bier and the bearers stood still, and he said, 'Young man, I tell you to get up.' And the dead man sat up and began to talk, and Jesus gave him to his mother" (Lk.7:11-15). Yeshua responded with *feeling*.

Another time when Yeshua visited his friends Martha and Mary, two sisters, he learned that their brother Lazarus had died. Mary came to Yeshua and "when Yeshua saw her weeping, and the Jews who had accompanied her also weeping, he was troubled in spirit and *moved by the deepest emotions*. 'Where have you laid him?' he asked. 'Lord, come and see,' they said. *Yeshua began to weep*, which caused the Jews to remark, 'See how much *he loved* him!" (Jn. 11:33-36). Yeshua was clearly a person with deep emotions, and showed them publicly.

Hence, it would seem that in category one Yeshua had not only the so-called "masculine" characteristics, but also the "feminine" ones.

## 2. Firm and Aggressive—Gentle and Peaceful

There is no question but that Yeshua was *firm*. He certainly was firm when he said to his chief follower Peter—in front of the rest of his followers(!): "Get behind me, Satan!" (Mk. 8:33). Yeshua's *aggressiveness* was expressed in several inflammatory statements: "I have come to bring fire to the earth, and how I wish it were blazing already!" (Lk. 12:49). "Do not suppose that I have come to bring peace to the earth: it is not peace I have come to bring, but a sword" (Mt. 10:34). "From John the Baptist's time until now the reign of God has suffered violence, and the violent take it by force" (Mt. 11:12). Yeshua was most aggressive in his verbal attack on his enemies among the scribes and Pharisees. *Six times* in a row he denounced them to their faces as frauds: "Alas for you, scribes and Pharisees, you frauds!" And he went on: "Alas for you, blind guides!...You blind men!...You blind guides! Straining out gnats and swallowing camels!...Alas for you, scribes and Pharisees, you hypocrites! You are like whitewashed tombs that look handsome on the outside, but inside are full of dead men's bones and every kind of corruption. In the same way you appear to people from the outside like good honest men, but inside you are full of hypocrisy and lawlessness.... Serpents, brood of vipers!" (Mt. 23:13-33).

Yeshua's firmness and aggressiveness was not simply in his word, but in his actions as well: "So they reached Jerusalem and he went into the Temple and began driving out those who were selling and buying there; he upset the tables of the money changers and the chairs of those selling pigeons. Nor would he allow anyone to carry anything through the Temple. And he taught them and said, 'Does not scripture say: My house will be called a house of prayer for all peoples? But you have turned it into a robber's den'" (Mk. 11:15-17).

On the other hand Yeshua spoke of *gentleness*. He described himself in an image that was the epitome of gentleness: "Jerusalem, Jerusalem, you that kill the prophets and stone those who are sent to you! How often have I longed to gather your children, as a hen gathers her brood under her wing"—note, Yeshua did not hesitate to use the feminine image of the hen to describe himself (Lk. 14:34). In the Sermon on the Mount he said, "Blessed are the *gentle:* they shall have the earth for their heritage" (Mt. 5:4). With extraordinary gentleness Yeshua spoke to the weary and weighted: "Come to me, all you who labor and are overburdened, and I will give you rest. Shoulder my yoke and learn from me, for I am *gentle* and humble in heart, and you will find rest for your souls. Yes, my yoke is easy and my burden light" (Mt. 11:28-30).

If a word other than "liberation" could also be said to sum up the life and message of Yeshua, it might be that pregnant Hebrew word, *shalom*, the fullness of active peace. In fact, it is recorded that at his birth angels sang, "Glory to God in high heaven, *peace* on earth to those on whom his favor rests" (Lk. 2:14). Time and again when Yeshua healed someone he said, "Your faith has saved you, go in *peace*." (Lk. 7:50; see also 8:48; Mk. 5:34). He instructed his disciples in peace: "Whatever house you go into, let your first words be, '*Peace* to this house!' And if a person of *peace* lives here, your *peace* will go and rest thereon" (Mt. 10:5-6). Yeshua went "far out" on peace; he taught, "When someone slaps you on one cheek, turn the other!" (Lk. 6:29). He promised much to the peace makers: "Blessed are the *peacemakers:* They shall be called the sons of God" (Mt. 5:9). To his followers he gave more: "I have told you this so that you may find *peace* in me.... *Peace* I bequeath to you, my own *peace* I give you, a *peace* the world cannot give, this is my gift to you" (Jn. 16:33; 14:27).

Obviously Yeshua was firm, aggressive *and* gentle, peaceloving; in category two he was both "masculine" and "feminine."

## 3. Justice—Mercy

Yeshua was a strong advocate of justice. To be just is to do what is right, and in society it is to follow the law (assuming the law is just). Yeshua insisted on scrupulously following the law: "Do not imagine I have come to abolish the Law or the Prophets. I have come not to abolish but to carry them out. I tell you solemnly, till heaven and earth disappear, not one dot, not one little stroke, shall disappear from the Law until its purpose is achieved. Therefore, whoever infringes even one of the least of these commandments and teaches others the same will be considered the least in the realm of heaven; but whoever keeps them and teaches them will be considered great in the realm of heaven" (Mt. 5:17-19). In the Beatitudes Yeshua promised, "Blessed are those who hunger and thirst for *justice;* they shall have their fill" (Mt. 5:6). Several times Yeshua spoke of the last judgment—where final justice would be meted out: "So will it be at the end of time. The Son of Humanity [Yeshua] will send his angels and they will gather out of his realm all things that provoke offenses and all who do evil, and throw them into the blazing furnace, where there will be weeping and grinding of teeth. Then the *just* will shine like the sun in the realm of their Father" (Mt. 13:41-43). Again: "This is how it will be at the end of time: the angels will appear and separate the wicked from the *just* to throw them into the blazing furnace where there will be weeping and grinding of teeth" (Mt. 13:49-50). And still again: "When the Son of Humanity comes in his glory...and all the nations will be assembled before him. Then he will separate them into two groups, as a shepherd separates sheep from goats. The sheep he will place on his right hand, the goats on his left.... These will go off to eternal punishment and the *just* to eternal life" (Mt. 25:31-33, 46). The epitaph on Yeshua's life, spoken by the Roman Centurion as Yeshua hung dead on the cross was: "Certainly this was a *just* man" (Lk. 23:47).

Nevertheless, Yeshua also said, "It is not the healthy who need the doctor, but the sick. Go and learn the meaning of the words: What I want is *mercy,* not sacrifice. And indeed I did not come to call the *just,* but sinners" (Mt. 9:13). Yeshua carried these words out, many times, just as we saw that he did with the woman who was caught in the act of adultery, an act punishable by death (Dt. 22:22ff.). He said: "'Has no one condemned you?' She said, 'No one, Lord.'" And Yeshua said, "Neither do I condemn you; go, and do not sin again'" (Jn.8:7-11). In the Beatitudes Yeshua promised, "Blessed are the *merciful:* They shall have *mercy* shown them" (Mt. 5:7). In a similar vein he also taught: "Be *merciful,* even as your Father is merciful. Judge not, and you will not be judged; condemn not, and you will not be condemned; *forgive,* and you will be forgiven" (Lk. 6:36-37). And how often should we forgive? That's what Peter wanted to know: "'Lord, how often shall my brother sin against me, and I *forgive* him? As many as seven times?' Yeshua said to him, 'I do not say to you seven times, but seventy times seven'" (Mt. 18:21-22).

Yeshua told many powerful parables, but perhaps his most moving was that of the Prodigal Son who took his inheritance before his father died, wasted it on wild living, and then finally crawled home in shame: "While he was still a long way off, his father caught sight of him and was deeply moved with *mercy*. He ran out to meet him, threw his arms around his neck, and kissed him. The son said to him, 'Father, I have sinned against God and against you; I no longer deserve to be called your son.' The father said.... 'Let us eat and celebrate, because this son of mine was dead and has come back to life. He was lost and is found'" (Lk. 15:20-24).

But in this matter of mercy and forgiveness Yeshua went beyond all his predecessors—and successors. He preached the unheard of doctrine of loving one's enemies: "You have learnt how it was said: You must love your neighbor and hate your enemy. But I say this to you: Love your enemies and pray for those who persecute you" (Mt. 5:43-44). Incredible *words*. But Yeshua *did* just that at the most critical moment of his life— his death: "When they reached the place called The Skull, they crucified him there and the two criminals also, one on the right, the other on the left. Yeshua said, 'Father, *forgive them*; they do not know what they are doing'" (Lk. 23:33-34). To the bitter end, Yeshua was a man of mercy.

As in the first two categories, so also in this, Yeshua strongly exemplified both the so-called "masculine" and "feminine" traits. Yeshua was a person of both justice and mercy, forgiveness.

## 4. Pride and Self-Confidence—Humility and Reserve

It might be thought that pride was foreign to Yeshua. But there is a kind of pride which, like its counterpart, humility, is simply truthfulness, affirming the good seen in oneself. A striking example of this pride occurred when a woman anointed Yeshua with some expensive perfumed ointment; there were complaints among his followers that the ointment should rather have been sold and the money given to the poor. "But Yeshua said, 'Leave her alone. Why are you upsetting her? What she has done for me is one of the good works. You have the poor with you always, and you can be kind to them whenever you wish, but you will not always have me'" (Mk. 14:6-9).

A perhaps even clearer example of this pride appeared when Yeshua made his triumphant entry into Jerusalem: "Great crowds of people spread their cloaks on the road, while others were cutting branches from the trees and spreading them in his path. The crowds who went in front of him and those who followed were all shouting: 'Hosanna to the Son of David! Blessings on him who comes in the name of the Lord! Hosanna in the highest heaven!' And when he entered Jerusalem, the whole city was in turmoil.... Some Pharisees in the crowd said to him, 'Teacher, rebuke your disciples.' He replied, 'If they were to keep silence, I tell you the very stones would cry out'" (Mt. 21:8-10; Lk. 19:39-40). The self-assurance and self-confidence Yeshua exhibited when dragged before the chief council of Israel was extraordinary. Only in someone who had a very firm grasp on himself could such be found; despite the violence and threats involved, Yeshua was clearly in control, in a way that usually happens only in spy thrillers: After being beaten "he was brought before their Council and they said to him, 'If you are the Messiah, tell us.' 'If I tell you,' he replied, 'you will not believe me, and if *I* question *you*, you will not answer. But from now on, the Son of Humanity will be seated at the right hand of the Power of God' (a quotation from Psalm 110:1). Then they said, 'So, you are the Son of God then?' He answered, 'It is you who say I am'" (Lk. 22:67-70).

If possible, even more self-assured was Yeshua's attitude later before Pilate, the notoriously cruel and bloodthirsty Roman governor of the area. The man had the power of release and a vicious death, and yet Yeshua had a steel control over himself—and his judge: Pilate said to Yeshua, '"Are you the king of the Jews?' Yeshua replied, 'Do you ask this of your own accord, or have others spoken to you about me?' Pilate answered, 'Am I a Jew? It is your own people and the chief priests who have handed you over to me: what have you done?' Yeshua replied, 'Mine is not a kingdom of this world; if my kingdom were of this world, my men would have fought to prevent my being surrendered to the Jews. But my kingdom is not of this kind.' 'So you are a king then?' said Pilate. 'It is you who say it' answered Yeshua. 'Yes, I am a king. I was born for this; I came into this world for this: to bear witness to the truth; and all who are on the side of truth listen to my voice.'... [Pilate said:] Surely you know I have power to release you and I have power to crucify you?' 'You would have no power over me,' replied Yeshua, 'if it had not been given you from above'" (Jn. 18:33-37; 19:10).

And yet, Yeshua is, rightly, known for teaching humility. As noted above, he said, "Learn from me, for I am gentle and *humble* in heart" (Mt. 11:29). He put flesh on this teaching with a story: "When someone invites you to a wedding feast, do not take your seat in the place of honor. A more distinguished person than you may have been invited, and the person who invited you both may come and say, 'Give up your place to this person.' And then, to your embarrassment, you would have to go and take the lowest place. No; when you are a guest, make your way to the lowest place and sit there, so that, when your host comes, he may say, 'My friend, move up higher.' In that way, everyone with you at the table will see you honored. For everyone who exalts himself will be humbled, and the one who *humbles* himself will be exalted" (Lk. 14:7-11).

Another story Yeshua told had much the same message. He spoke of a Pharisee in the Temple who bragged to God about all his virtues, and of a hated tax collector who beat his breast and said, "God, be merciful to me, a sinner." "This man, I tell you, went home again at rights with God; the other did not. For everyone who exalts himself will be humbled, but the one who *humbles* himself will be exalted" (Lk. 18:9-14).

Yeshua paradoxically also often taught his followers *reserve*. For ex ample, he said: "Be careful not to parade your good deeds before people to attract their notice." Or, "When you give alms, do not have it trumpeted before you.... but when you give alms, your left hand must not know what your right is doing; your almsgiving must be secret." And further, "When you pray, do not imitate the hypocrites; they love to say their prayers standing up in the synagogues.... But when you pray, go to your private room and, when you have shut your door, pray to your Father who is in that secret place" (Mt. 6:1-6).

From this evidence, and still more in the gospels, we would have to conclude that Yeshua combined the so-called "masculine" traits of pride and self-confidence with the supposedly "feminine" characteristics of humility and reserve.

### 5. Provider of Security—Need for Security

The pattern that has emerged by now is so clear it hardly seems necessary to continue with a thorough analysis. Let us make it even briefer than above.

It was to Yeshua that his many followers flocked to find the *security* of the meaning of human life; of whom Peter said, "Lord, to whom shall we go? You have the words of eternal life" (Jn. 6:67); who said of himself, "I am the bread of life. He who comes to me will never be hungry." (Jn. 6:35). Yet it was also the same Yeshua who sent his disciples out with "no purse, no haversack, no sandals" (Lk. 10:4); who said to them, "That is why I am telling you not to worry about your life and what to eat, nor about your body and how you are to clothe it" (Lk. 12:22); who said of himself, "Foxes have holes and the birds of the air have their nests, but the Son of Humanity has nowhere to lay his head" (Lk. 9:58); and who in the end felt a crushing need for security in his God: "My God, my God, why have you forsaken me?" (Mk. 15:34). Yeshua both provided, and needed, security.

## 6. Organization—People

Briefly, in the final category, note Yeshua's concern with *organization and structure* by recalling his carefully choosing his followers, his apostles—twelve to match symbolically the twelve tribes of Israel ("You will sit on thrones to judge the twelve tribes of Israel," Lk. 22:30), the painful and painstaking instruction of his followers, his sending out of the seventy disciples like "lead men" in a political campaign today "to all the towns and places he himself was to visit" (Lk. 10:1). But there is also Yeshua's intense concern with individual *persons,* his healing of numerous miserable people, lepers, blind, lame, paralytics, etc., etc., even the dead(!), his affection for despised individuals, like the tax collector Zacchaeus (Lk. 19:1ff.), the "sinful" woman (Lk. 7:36ff.), the adulterous woman (Jn. 8:1ff.). There is also Yeshua's special concern for *children*—in fact, the holding of them up as a model: "People were bringing little children to him, for him to touch them. The disciples turned them away, but when Yeshua saw this he was indignant and said to them, 'Let the little children come to me; do not stop them; for it is to such as these that the reign of God belongs. I tell you solemnly, anyone who does not welcome the reign of God like a child will never enter it.' *Then he put his arms around them,* laid his hands on them and gave them his blessing" (Mk. 10:13-16).

## 7. Conclusion

There is no question: the evidence shows overwhelmingly that Yeshua had the full range of so-called "feminine" and "masculine" characteristics in all the categories. What conclusion does that suggest? For one, it suggests that the division of characteristics by sex is quite artificial, false. Yeshua would have been less than a full human being if he had only the so-called masculine set. In fact, if he had had only one set exclusively he would have been so lopsided as to have been an inhuman monster. Unfortunately this sex-role distortion has too often happened to the *image* of Yeshua in Christianity, past and present. At different times and places Yeshua has been seen solely as the great ruler of the world, a stern just judge whose favor must be curried through his more sympathetic mother. At other times Yeshua has been projected as all-feeling, "loving," or according to the "Jesus freaks," a person who "saves," without any just judgment involved. But Yeshua was not just so-called "masculine" or "feminine." He was fully human. The model of how to live an authentically human life, of how to attain "salvation," that the Yeshua of the gospels presents is not one that fits the masculine stereotype, which automatically relegates the "softer," "feminine" traits to women as being beneath the male—nor indeed is it the opposite stereotype. Rather, it is an egalitarian model. Thus the same message that Yeshua taught in his words and dealings with women, namely, egalitarianism between women and men, was also taught by his own androgynous life style.

What has often happened to the image of Yeshua in our society also tends to happen to most of us to a greater or lesser degree. Women are made to think they must cultivate only their "womanly" traits and avoid their "manly" ones, and the converse for men. But the liberating "Good News" of what Yeshua thought, taught and wrought is that to be an authentic human we must reject the false division of traits by sex. Thus we will come to know, and love, our true, integrated self and will thereby be able to see our oneness with all our fellow humans (and most especially the oppressed), with all nature, and ultimately with the Source of all.

## Notes

1. Hanna Wolff, *Jesus der Mann* (Stuttgart: Radius, 1979), pp. 80f. While Dr. Wolff is very insightful regarding the psychological character balance of Yeshua and his lack of a hostile animus, she herself retains an extraordinary animus against all things Jewish. Moreover, she not only is aware of and rejects the work of Christian and Jewish scholars who are recovering the manifold dimensions of the Jewishness of Yeshua, she positively rails against them. Not being a Scripture scholar herself, or anything near it, she simply polemically insists that their work *must* be mistaken. In this she continues the age-old Christian anti-Judaism, and perhaps also the modern German anti-Jewish animus. As is well known, this animus is especially dangerous.

2. In rabbinic writings, e.g., the Mishnah (codified 200 C.E.), the Tosephta (codified just afterwards), the Palestinian Talmud (400 C.E.), the Babylonian Talmud (500 C.E.), there are many references to persons and things to as far back as 200 B.C.E. Thus, as discussed in notes above, in many matters we can know what the rabbis of the time of Yeshua taught, even though caution must be exercised since the later codifier might have adjusted texts for his own purposes. Nevertheless, until cogent arguments and evidence are brought forth that substantial revision did occur in the pertinent passages, good scholarship dictates that the available texts be utilized with due care. For a broad treatment of this subject, see Leonard Swidler, *Women in Judaism. The Status of Women in Formative Judaism* (Metuchen, NJ: Scarecrow Press, 1976), and Leonard Swidler, *Biblical Affirmations of Woman* (Philadelphia: Westminster Press, 1979).

3. *Mishnah*, Sota 3,4.

4. *Talmud*, bKid. 33b; *Mishnah*, Ber. 3,3.

5. *Talmud*, bBer. 20b.

6. *Tosephta*, Ber. 7,18; *Talmud*, pBer. 13b; bMen. 43b.

7. *Mishnah*, Abot 3,6.

8. See Josephus, *Antiquities*, XV, 418f.; *Jewish War*, V, 5, par. 198 f.; *Mishnah*, Middoth 2,5.

9. See Eliezer L. Sukenik, *Ancient Synagogues in Palestine and Greece* (London, 1934), pp. 47 ff. See also Bernadette J. Brooten, *Women Leaders in the Ancient Synagogue* (Chico, CA: Scholars Press, 1982), where the author raises serious questions about

how early the physical division of men and women was reflected in the synagogue architecture. By the nature of the issue, she cannot offer positive proof that there was no such architectural separation (which, as we know definitely existed later, and still up to the present in some synagogues); she does however make the usual claims that it did exist at the time of Yeshua less than certain. Nevertheless, looking at all the evidence, I am persuaded that it is more likely that women and men were separated in the synagogues at the time of Yeshua.

Dr. Brooten also argues for some modicum of leadership roles for women in ancient Judaism, albeit as exceptions. Her scholarship is superb and her case solid. But the exceptions that she adduces, important as they are as "useable history" for women, remain so much just that, that they become the proverbial "exceptions that prove the rule"; the general description of ancient Jewish women as largely officially excluded from leadership roles still stands.

10. *Mishnah*, Aboth 1,5.

11. *Talmud*, b Ber. 43b.

12. Ibid.

13. *Mishnah*, Shab. 4,1; *Talmud*, bB.K. 88a; Josephus, *Antiquities*, IV, 219.

14. Philo, *Flaccus*, 89; *De specialibus legibus*, III, 172.

15. Philo, *De specialibus legibus*, III, 169.

16. *Talmud*, bKid. 82b; cf. also bSan. 100b.

17. *Talmud*, bNid. 31b.

18. Ibid.

19. *Mishnah*, Terum 15; *Talmud*, pKid. 4,66b, 32; Soferim 41a in *The Minor Tractates of the Talmud*, ed. by A. Cohen (London, 1971), p. 288.

20. *Midrash*, GnR. 45, 5.

21. Addressing all women Tertullian says: "And do you not know that you are (each) an Eve? The sentence of God on this sex of yours lives in this age: the guilt must of necessity live too. You are the devil's gateway; you are the unsealer of that (forbidden) tree: you are the first deserter of the divine law: you are she who persuaded him whom the devil was not valiant enough to attack. You destroyed so easily God's image, man. On account of your desert—that is, death—even the Son of God had to die." *De cultu feminarum* 1.1, in *The Fathers of the Church*, vol. 40, pp. 117f.

22. Origen, *Selecta in Exodus* XVIII.17, in Migne, *Patrologia Graeca*, vol. 12, cols. 296f.

23. Epiphanius wrote: "For the female sex is easily seduced, weak, and without much understanding. The devil seeks to vomit out his disorder through women.... We wish to apply masculine reasoning and destroy the folly of these women." *Adversus Collyridianos*, in Migne, *Patrologia Graeca*, vol. 42, cols. 740f.

24. Josephus states: "The woman, says the law, is in all things inferior to the man." *Against Apion*, II,201.

25. For a discussion of this "wandering" story of Yeshua and the adulteress see Swidler, *Biblical Affirmations*, pp. 185f., 250f., 275f., where the evidence for its having first been recorded by a woman "evangelist" is discussed.

26. This whole essay of course attempts to present evidence sustaining this point. In this regard it is interesting to note that there are at least two early New Testament textual variants which directly accuse Yeshua of running counter to the culture and "leading women astray." In Luke 23:5 there is a variant manuscript reading attested to by the fourth-century Palestinian-born Church father Epiphanius: The chief priests said to

Pilate of Yeshua, "He is inflaming the people with his teaching all over Judea; it has come all the way from Galilee, where he started, down to here"—to which Epiphanius' attested text adds, "and he has turned our children and wives away from us for they are not bathed as we are, nor do they purify themselves (*et filios nostros et uxores avertit a nobis, non enim baptizantur sicut nos nec se mundant*)." The second text is even earlier, the first half of the second century, when some of the New Testament itself was still being written. It is attested to by Marcion (d. 160 A.D.) and occurs in Luke 23:2: "They began their accusation by saying, 'We found this man inciting our people to a revolt, opposing payment of the tribute to Caesar'"—to which Marcion's attested text adds, "leading astray the women and the children (*kai apostrephonta tas gynaikas kai ta tekna*)." For these variant texts and references see Eberhard Nestle, ed., *Novum Testamentum Graece et Latine* (Stuttgart, 1954), p. 221, and Roger Gryson, *The Ministry of Women in the Early Church* (Collegeville, MN: Liturgical Press, 1976), p. 126.

27. For a brief discussion of the implications of the Greek word used for "ministering," *diakoneo*, see Swidler, *Biblical Affirmations*, pp. 194f. There is also a specific reference in the Acts of the Apostles to a woman by name as a disciple of Yeshua: "At Jaffa there was a woman disciple (*mathetria*) called Tabitha, or Dorcas in Greek" (Acts 9:36).

28. Cf. also Mk. 15:40f. and Mt. 27:55f. where the women are also reported to have "ministered" (*diekonoun*) to Yeshua. A fascinating second-century Gnostic document refers to the seven holy women named in the gospels as disciples on a par with the Twelve Apostles: "After he had risen from the dead, when they came, the twelve disciples (*mathetes*) and seven women who had followed him as disciples (*matheteuein*), into Galilee,...there appeared to them the Redeemer." *Sophia Jesu Christi*, in E. Hennecke and W. Schneemelcher, *New Testament Apocrypha* (Philadelphia: Westminster Press, 1963), vol. 1, p. 246. See Swidler, *Biblical Affirmations*, pp. 195f. for further similar texts.

29. For further discussion of sexually parallel stories in the New Testament see Swidler, *Biblical Affirmations*, pp. 164ff.

# CHAPTER 4

# Can One Gain Salvation Only Through Yeshua the Christ?

Christians believe that it is through Yeshua, who is the Christ, the meeting point of the human and the divine, that they come to live a life of wholeness, holiness, of salvation. He is the door (Jn. 10:9) through which they enter into the knowledge and full love of their selves, neighbors, nature and the Source of all. The question I would like to reflect on here is whether in order for Christians to act with integrity with their tradition they have to claim that the only way any human being can attain wholeness, holiness, salvation, is through following the way of Yeshua the Christ? I believe that a Christian need not, indeed ought not, make such an exclusivistic claim, even though perhaps the vast majority of Christians have done so in the past.

Humanity is slowly but inexorably emerging out of the age of monologue into the age of dialogue. Hence, in light of our new, deeper dialogic understanding of truth we must think through again the vital points of our traditions, starting at their sources. For us Christians that means especially the Scriptures, and particularly the New Testament, for it is there that we find our foundation, our founder, Yeshua the Christ. Among other things, we need to reflect on those passages which have become the bases for our subsequent exclusivistic claims that salvation can come only through Yeshua the Christ—though interestingly, Yeshua himself says, according to John, that "salvation is from the Jews" (Jn. 4:22).

## 1. "God Was Reconciled to the World through Christ"

Therefore, as a way to proceed with the question I wish to take one such passage from the New Testament that has been understood in an exclusivistic Christian manner and reflect on its meaning with the aid of contemporary critical thought and scholarship. In so doing, a number of the considerations raised will also be applicable to the other places in the New Testament which have been used in an exclusivistic manner, although each one would also deserve a full analysis of the text within its own context. Nevertheless, I believe the way will have been shown how to authentically understand these passages, particularly now in the beginning of the dialogic age.

A word of caution, however: Whenever a major paradigm shift occurs in a culture or community, there will also be major resistance, and in the beginning this resistance will be within our own breasts.

I would like to look at the statement of Paul where he says that "God was reconciling the world to himself through Christ" (II Cor. 5:19—see also Rom. 5:10f.). This has often been taken to mean that only through Yeshua the Christ can a person be reconciled to God, and obviously not being reconciled to God means that one cannot live a life of wholeness, holiness, salvation. Is this Christian exclusivistic understanding correct?

It is important here to once again recall what was stressed earlier, namely, that when trying to understand the writings of Paul we must bear in mind that we are dealing with a believing Jew, indeed by his own word, a Pharisaic Jew, who was also at home in the Hellenistic-Jewish thought world. To not read him this way—as unfortunately Christians (and, following them, Jews!) traditionally too often have not, until most recently— is to mis-read him.

In this statement in his letter to the Corinthians Paul is obviously talking about something that far transcends the every-day life experience that we have of reality. Clearly then, he is not going to be able to use language in its normal, every-day sense. However, like all human beings, he will nevertheless have to use the one language that we have, namely, human language, with all of its limitations, formed by every-day experiences—and then perhaps at most, extend it out from that every-day experience to lend it additional variations of meaning.[1]

Thus, although Paul necessarily used every-day language, he sometimes used it in a way that was quite common in his time in order to convey meanings which went far beyond our every-day experience of things: such use of language very often is called *mythic, that is, the use of a connected set of images that points to a meaning beyond the surface meaning—like a metaphor.* And that is what Paul is doing here. That means that his language will *sound* as if he were describing in a very empirical, perhaps even physical, ontological, manner what he understood *really* to have happened on a different level in the relationship between the world and God in the Christ event.

The image that is projected by Paul is as if somehow the world, meaning mainly humanity, was in a way pointed in the wrong direction, namely, away from God—who existed in a transcendent fashion, that is, outside of the world. Then God worked through Christ who, as it were, reached his huge hand up and grasped the world by the scruff of its neck and turned it around so that it was facing God once again. Thus, there was a sort of ontological, cosmic "reconciling of the world with God through Christ."

But of course this is a trans-physical, mythic, metaphorical image. Paul was not so naive as to think that he was in fact empirically describing the way things really are physically with this language in the same way as he might describe the various parts of a tent, how they are related to each other, what materials they are made of, etc. (as a professional tent maker he presumably must have done this, often quite well). Rather, he was attempting to communicate some insight which would contribute to religion, that is, an "explanation of the meaning of life, and how to live accordingly." This is what mythic stories are supposed to do. Just what was this insight contributing to the "explanation of the meaning of life" that Paul was trying to communicate with this mythic image? It seems to me that it can be explained as follows:

Paul obviously had a profound experience of Jesus Christ, even though he never met him personally while he, Yeshua, was alive on earth. This experience of Jesus Christ was for Paul quite obviously a breakthrough kind of experience, or, said in other words, a "turn-around," a *metanoia*, conversion, kind of experience. Through it he felt that he now had a profoundly positive kind of relationship with the ultimate meaning of life for him, which he called God, and this for him new, profoundly positive relationship, came through his encounter with Jesus Christ. For Paul, Jesus Christ provided the opportunity, the occasion, the means to have this positive relationship with the ultimate meaning of life, God. Put in other words, Paul was much more interested in soteriology, "salvation-ology," than Christology; Paul was much more concerned about "Christ's incarnation in Christians" than in "God's incarnation in Christ."[2]

In similar fashion, for other Christians Jesus Christ has also been this means of attaining a profoundly positive relationship with the ultimate meaning of life, God. From Jesus Christ, or more precisely, Yeshua, Christians learn that the ultimate meaning of life is to stand in the center of one's being and turn and reach outward; it is to love, to reach out beyond oneself to the good, that is, to being, to all that exists. Primarily for human beings this means other persons, but it also includes all beings, and ultimately the Source, Sustainer and Goal of all being, whom Christians and many others call God. (Non-theists, like Theravada Buddhists, may prefer to use terms such as, "universe" or "nature"—perhaps not unlike that school of Western thought that spoke of "God, that is, Nature," *Deus sive Natura.*)

This is not in any way self-destructive, for as was noted before and pointed out by Yeshua when he cited from the Hebrew Bible, we are to love our neighbor as our self. We can love our neighbor, that is, others, then, only to the extent that we truly love ourselves. Authentic self-love and authentic love of the other, are not only not mutually exclusive, they are necessarily mutually inclusive.

There is of course much, much more to the further understanding of the living out of this central insight that Christians claim to find in the life of Yeshua. As remarked earlier, Christians believe, that is, they are convinced, that in this man Yeshua of Nazareth this central insight into the meaning of human life, and the attendant insights and implications, were so fully exemplified and lived out to the point of a self-emptying, agonizing death for the sake of his friends that they feel compelled to use language which speaks of the meeting of the human and the divine in him. At any rate, by looking at Yeshua, by encountering him, Christians claim that they are thereby enabled to have a profound positive relationship with God. In other words, they are "reconciled to God."

## 2. Paradigm-shift in Language and Thought

Christians, further, are convinced that the inflow of insights as to the meaning of life was so overwhelming in Yeshua that to express this perception they had to turn to hyperbolic language, language which was metaphorical, poetic, for this kind of language normally is what human beings must use when trying to express something which transcends every-day language. This is the same point made earlier when speaking of Paul's use of what I called mythic language. The Catholic theologian David Tracy expresses the same idea when he uses the term "limit-language":

All authentic limit-language seems to be initially and irretrievably a symbolic and metaphorical one. Insofar as

> the hidden dimension of an ultimate limit is not merely hidden
> but not even expressible in the language of the everyday (as no-
> *thing,* no object in the world alongside other objects), that lan-
> guage retains the linguistic structure of metaphor and symbols....
> even *explicitly* religious language (e.g., the language of the scrip-
> tures or of the Christian myths) is intrinsically symbolic and
> metaphorical limit-language.[3]

Hence, recalling what we had said earlier, Christians eventually began to speak of Yeshua of Nazareth as the meeting point of the divine and the human, so that later, in the fourth and fifth centuries when Christianity had become the state religion of the Roman empire and had largely embraced the Hellenistic thought world and means of conceptualization, orthodox Christians began to speak of the "God-man." Unfortunately for subsequent Christians, and for the rest of the world, the profound insight that the first Christians had in their liberating encounter with Yeshua of Nazareth was now translated out of its poetic, metaphorical language into Hellenistic empirical, ontological language in a manner that took the original language to also be empirical, ontological. Not to perceive that almost all the original language of the first Christians as expressed in the New Testament was in fact poetic, metaphorical, when speaking in its most ecstatic terms about the significance and meaning of Yeshua of Nazareth,[4] was a profound misjudgment.

The fundamental drive in this "ontologizing" move in understanding the initially metaphorical language speaking about Yeshua, of course, as was noted in an earlier chapter, is the need to give expression to the experiencing of the trans-empirical, the trans-cendent, which for Christians happens through Yeshua, just as for Buddhists it happens through Siddharta Gautama. Nevertheless, at the same time it is essential to be aware what kind of language is being used if one is to understand it properly.

Paul himself, the great preacher of the "proclaimed *Christos*," made it crystal clear that for the most part he—necessarily—used metaphorical language when speaking of *Christos* and his relationship to God (*ho theos*) when in his first letter to the Corinthians he noted that in the end *Christos* (here referred to as the son, *ho huios*) would not stand supreme over all, as if he himself were God, *ho theos,* but would submit himself to God: "The son (*ho huios*) himself will submit to him who submitted all things to him so that God (*ho theos*) may be all things in all" (I Cor. 15:28).

Hans Küng speaks in a different but nevertheless similar manner when he writes that Yeshua "*is* in human form God's 'Word,' 'Will,' 'Son.'" However, this statement must not be misunderstood. Even New Testament talk about the Father and the Son must not be understood as a two-god teaching, a bi-theism, and then tri-theism. "No, God is for Jesus and thus also for Christians of all times always the one and only. There is, even in the Bible, no other god outside of God!... The Son is not God the Father, and God the Father is not the Son.... The historical person of Jesus Christ stands for God, manifests him, definitively reveals him."[5]

However, given the difference between the Semitic and Hellenistic thought worlds, perhaps such a misperception was unavoidable. The Hellenistic Christians had to try to understand the meaning of Yeshua in their own thought categories. Since the Hellenistic world did not have a historical, relational view of truth, but rather an absolutist one, it was almost impossible for it to conceive of authentically valid statements about the meaning of life in categories other than its own absolutist, ontological ones, assuming that all true statements about the meaning of life could be properly expressed only in such categories. Of course, in today's mental world with its historical, relational understanding of truth, we need not, indeed *may not,* remain thus limited. We must attempt to recapture the original "historical," significance of what Yeshua thought, taught and wrought and express that in contemporary historical, deabsolutized, critical-thought categories.[6]

Even in the New Testament, however, the early Christians spoke of Yeshua as if he were not only *a* possible way to learn the meaning of human life, and thereby to become reconciled with God, but they felt that in comparison with all other possibilities he was so vastly far in advance of, so radically better than, the others that they spoke of him in absolute language. Or at least, they did so at times. Again, it becomes apparent that they were speaking in hyperbolic terms—just as when Yeshua spoke of the eye that scandalized one, one should pluck it out, everyone understood him not to mean an actual physical destruction of one's eye; this was a metaphorical way of communicating a profoundly important religious message. For, it must be recalled that in fact the very central notions and insights that Yeshua was communicating, e.g., those of love of God and love of neighbor as being the two greatest commandments, were not exclusively his, but rather were precisely the central pillars not only of the ancient Israelite religion, but also quite specifically those of (Pharisaic) proto-rabbinic Judaism. Hence, in other words, as discussed before, Yeshua and his followers, including the writers of the New Testament, were Jews, and hence thought and spoke Jewishly, i.e., metaphorically rather than ontologically.

### 3. Modern Paradigm-shift

While there was a shift in paradigms of how one perceived and understood the world at the very beginning of Christianity from the Jewish paradigm to the Hellenistic one, today we are undergoing a paradigm shift within our own culture. It was relatively simple for the gentiles to take over the Jewish Good News of Yeshua and translate it into their own Hellenistic paradigm, or mode of understanding and expression—with, nevertheless, as we have seen, some severely damaging distortions resulting from their not noticing that they were moving from metaphorical to ontological language. However, as mentioned earlier, when a paradigm shift occurs within a culture it always encounters deep, dogged resistance and a great deal of pain is undergone before the new paradigm is finally accepted—for example, the shift in science from the geocentric to the heliocentric paradigm of understanding the universe took over a hundred years from Copernicus (d. 1543) to beyond Galileo (d. 1642) was not without much suffering, as the latter could testify.

Whereas the notion of truth in the West was largely absolute, static, monologic or exclusive up to the last century, it has subsequently become deabsolutized, dynamic and dialogic—in a word—relational. This "new" view of truth came about in at least six different but closely related ways.

0) Before the nineteenth century in Europe truth, that is, a statement about reality, was conceived in quite an absolute, static, exclusivistic either-or manner. It was thought that if something was true at some time or other, it was always true, and not only in regard to empirical facts but also in regard to the meaning of things. This is a *classicist* or *absolutist* view of truth.

1) In the nineteenth century scholars came to perceive all statements about the truth of the meaning of something partially as products of their historical circumstances; only by placing the truth statements in their historical situations, their historical *Sitz im Leben,* could they be properly understood. All statements about the meaning of things were seen to be deabsolutized in terms of time. This is a *historical* view of truth.

2) Later it was noted that we ask questions so as to obtain knowledge, truth, according to which we want to live; this is a *praxis* or *intentional* view of truth, that is, a statement has to be understood in relationship to the action-oriented intention of the thinker.

3) Early in this century Karl Mannheim developed what he called the sociology of knowledge, which points out that every statement about the truth of the meaning of something was *perspectival,* for all reality is perceived, and spoken of, from the cultural, class, sexual, and so forth perspective of the perceiver.

4) Ludwig Wittgenstein and many other thinkers have discovered something of the limitations of human language. Every description of reality can necessarily be only partial for although reality can be seen from an almost limitless number of perspectives, human language can express things from only one, or perhaps a very few, perspectives at once. This *partialness* and limitedness of all language is necessarily greatly intensified when one attempts to speak of the transcendent, which by definition "goes-beyond."

5) The contemporary science of hermeneutics stresses that all knowledge is interpreted knowledge. That means that in all knowledge *I* come to know something; the object comes into me in a certain way, namely, through the lens that I use to perceive it. As Thomas Aquinas said,

"things known are in the knower according to the mode of the knower." This is an *interpretative* view of truth.

6) Still further, reality can "speak" to me only with the language that I give it. The "answers" that I receive back from reality will always be in the language, the thought categories, of the questions I put to it. If the answers I receive are sometimes confused and unsatisfying, then I probably need to learn to speak a more appropriate language when I put questions to reality. If, for example, I ask the question, "How far is yellow?" of course I will receive an non-sense answer. Or if I ask questions about living things in mechanical categories, I will receive confusing and unsatisfying answers. So too will I receive confusing and unsatisfying answers to questions about human sexuality if I use categories that are solely physical- biological: Witness the absurdity of the answer that birth control is forbidden by the natural law—the question falsely assumes that the nature of humanity is merely physical-biological. This understanding of truth is a *dialogic* understanding.

In short, our understanding of truth and reality has been undergoing a radical shift. This new paradigm which is being born understands all statements about reality, especially about the meaning of things, to be historical, intentional, perspectival, partial, interpretative and dialogic. It is bearing this paradigm shift in mind that we must now proceed with our analysis.

## 4. Other Paths to God

Returning to the question of "being reconciled to God," logically one would have to ask next, What about other great religious leaders in the history of humankind? For example, are not many of the insights found in the core teachings of the "Fathers" of Rabbinic Judaism very helpful to all persons in leading them to understand more fully the meaning of human life, that is, to "be reconciled to God"? Cannot similar things be said of the profoundly beautiful and insightful teachings of Moses, Mohammed, Gautama, and others? To be sure, one would have to say, Yes—which is precisely what is also said by the Muslim thinker Hasan Askari:

> As far as the subjects of the finality claim (Gautama, Jesus or *Muhammed*) are concerned...if they point to themselves (which they cannot do in terms of the metaphor they employ, for that will involve contradiction), all of them are false; and if they point to the Beyond (which is precisely what the mataphor is all about), all of them are true.[7]

Nevertheless, Christians are those who are persuaded that in Yeshua of Nazareth one finds the full explanation, the living out of the meaning of life—a reconciliation with God. They claim that all human beings in fact *could* find the meaning of life through Yeshua of Nazareth. Therefore they make a universal claim that Yeshua of Nazareth provides salvation for all human beings, that is, he provides a way to "be reconciled with God" for all human beings. However, at the same time, one must also recognize that not all human beings *in fact* have been, are, or will be in a position to receive this insight, to be "reconciled with God through Christ." They may, in fact, have other paths by which they come to this insight, to this "reconciliation."

But what then of the claim of the early Christians about the universal salvific significance of Jesus Christ? Could it not be understood to be of *potentially* universal salvific significance? The insights and exemplification of how to live an authentic human life in a proper relationship to God given by Yeshua are believed by Christians in fact to be the true way to be fully human, to be in a right relationship to God, the ultimate meaning of life.

But, is it not possible that there could be various ways in which to express these insights, not only in terms of ideas, teachings, stories, etc., but also in various practices, patterns of social relationship, and the like? That would mean there would be all sorts of ways of teaching and passing on these profound insights into the meaning of life. These would then coalesce around certain outstanding teachers, and form various social patterns or structures, which we call religions or ideologies. This is not to say, of course, that everything taught and practiced in every religion or ideology is necessarily authentically human, authentically a "reconciliation of the world with God," as Christians believe they find in Yeshua. This is not any more likely than that everything Christians have taught and practiced in the past two thousand years has been authentic in its expression of the meaning of life, has been in fact true to the insights and example given by Yeshua.

There are a number of other considerations that lead to the same conclusions. For example, it should be noted that "christological statements should be regarded as belonging not to the language of philosophy, science or dogmatics, but rather to the language of confession and testimony."[8] Or to use the terminology of Krister Stendhal, they are in "religious language.... love language, caressing language."[9] One can attempt to translate love language into philosophical language, poetry into prose (though there will be an inevitable loss), but it would be a gross error and distortion to treat love language, poetry itself, as if it were actually philosophical prose.

That has happened too often in Christianity (and other religions as well), with the all too frequent fateful result that the message is distorted, and sometimes even destroyed; that has been especially true of the statements of the first followers of Yeshua, as discussed above.[10]

Furthermore, the ancient world lived within the mentality of classicist culture where the view of truth was static, absolute, exclusivistically either-or—as was outlined above. Hence, if they believed something about Yeshua was true, it therefore *had* to be unchanging, absolute, exclusive, for that was the nature of truth, as they understood it. But with the paradigm or model shift in the modern critical worldview to the historical, inten-tional, perspectival, partial, interpretative, dialogic views of truth, critical Christians are now able to, *must,* affirm the salvific, "reconciling," truth about Yeshua—what he thought, taught and wrought—without being abso-lutistic and exclusivistic.

Paul Knitter pointed out that the early Christians were certainly aware that there were many truth claims in the world around them. However, "they felt that if any one of these claims really were true, it had to either conquer or absorb the others. That is what truth did. Unavoidably, then, when they encountered the overwhelming truth of Jesus, they would have to describe it as the only or the final truth." But, Knitter added, in today's world of historical consciousness, "coupled with a new experience of plu-ralism it seems possible for Christians to feel and announce the saving truth about Jesus and his message without the requirements of classicist culture, i.e., without having to insist that Jesus' truth is either exclusive or inclusive of all other truth."[11]

Still further, it must be remembered that the world of the Way of Yeshua was a world of Jewish eschatological apocalypticism: the end of the world was imminent, as was also the "second coming." The reign of God which Yeshua preached was about to be fulfilled through him. As a result, one of the earliest community reflections on the meaning of Yeshua was a "Maranatha Christology."[12] Hence, there could have been no thought at all about the possibility of other saviors; there was no time for them to happen. Quick, get ready now!

But when the final end of this world by its transformation into the reign of God through the "second coming" of Yeshua did not happen, the final-ity of the *end-time* was shifted to the *center* of history, as was analyzed by Rosemary Ruether.[13] Yeshua as the *final,* eschatological prophet was sim-ply moved to be the *center* of history: A shift from an apocalyptic to a classicist worldview. Again, with the passing of both of these worldviews the saving significance of Yeshua can, must, be expressed without its abso-lutistic and exclusivistic "protective coloring." Just as Christians made the shift from the apocalyptic to the classicist worldview, so too must they make the shift to the critical, relational worldview—with at least all the painful reconceptualization that the earlier shift involved.

Perhaps ironically the claim on the part of the earliest followers of Yeshua of which we have any documentation, the community behind the "Q" document, "The Sayings of Jesus," imbedded in the Synoptic Gospels, is not an exclusivistic salvational claim for Yeshua. Rather, that claim is made for God as God "faces the world," that is, the spirit of God: "And whoever says a word against the son of humanity (a term Yeshua used to refer to himself) will be forgiven; but whoever blasphemes against the holy Spirit will not be forgiven" (Mt. 12: 32; Lk. 12: 10). "Jesus as an ordinary human being can be spoken against and those who do so can be for-given.... but no one may be forgiven who blasphemes against God himself. This passage implies the very human origins of Jesus that we noted...be-fore his adoption by God."[14] In other words, not following Yeshua is forgivable, but not following the *spirit,* that is, not following one's cultural and inner in*spirat*ion, is not.

If there is any validity in these reflections, it should be apparent that Christians need not, should not, take a condemnatory attitude toward non-Christians, particularly those who are adherents of other religions or ide-ologies, for fear that they would be disloyal to their Christian commitment. Rather, they would be disloyal to their Christian commitment (that is, *ef-fectively* to preach the Good News to today's, critical-thinking, world, i.e., in a language which is dynamic and dialogic) if they did not seek to recog-nize the same truths, the same insights, wherever they find them. This immediately implies that Christians ought to take a stance not of debate, but rather of dialogue with non-Christians. In this dialogue they will doubtless learn that there are many valuable insights in their own Christian traditions which they had overlooked, or suppressed, or distorted, and they will have been brought to this re-discovery of their own treasures through finding those very same insights held forth in another religion or ideology in exemplary fashion.

Moreover, is it not also possible that they will discover in another relig-ious, ideological tradition insights which in fact do not seem to have been expressed in their own Christian tradition? If they can resist the tempta-tion to be doctrinaire and triumphalistic, they will have to say, yes, it is possible; we can hope to gain truly new insights into the meaning of life.

What does this do to the Christian notion that Yeshua the Christ is somehow the fullness of what it means to be human? For one thing, it would be said that presumably none of the new insights gathered would in fact run contrary to what had already been exemplified ("revealed," to use theological language "from above") in Yeshua the Christ.

Further, one can speak of a development, an unfolding, an evolution. One can take the language of a Teilhard de Chardin and speak of moving from the Alpha to the Omega point. Is it not the case that even the early Christians spoke of *another* coming of the Christ? Surely another coming is not going to be identical with the first coming. If it were, it would not be another coming; it would be the first coming. There will of course be profound similarities, but if it is to be another, then there must also be some differences.

Might not these "new insights" constitute part of these differences? If in fact Christians come to be persuaded that Mohammed and Marx, for example, provided some "new insights," might they not be seen as part of the "other coming"? Does the second coming of Christ have to be seen and understood only in terms of being at a specific time at the end of history? Obviously that is not necessary, for here we are clearly again dealing with metaphorical, hyperbolic, poetic, mythic language. Talk of the eschaton is clearly beyond our every-day experience. However, cannot the events within history be taken to be stages toward, even constitutive elements leading to, that eschaton, that Omega point, to again use Teilhardian language? If so, then there need be no opposition ultimately between the Christian understanding of how the world is "reconciled to God through Christ" and how many people will in fact experience this reconciliation to God, this learning of the ultimate meaning of human life, through means other than Jesus Christ, Yeshua.

## 5. Expanded Use of the Term "Christ"

John Cobb has pointed out that until the nineteenth century it was assumed that Yeshua expressly affirmed his own divinity. However,

> The creative transformation that is the history of New Testament scholarship step by step removed from our understanding of the real Jesus all such claims about himself. It participated centrally thereby in the radical humanization of the Christian image of Christ that has dominated the recent history of the understanding of incarnation.[15]

That has led to the possibility—and, as I have argued, the necessity—of making the historical Yeshua, the fully human being, the standard of what it means to be Christian. However, the power of the impact of Yeshua on his followers was so great that "it gave rise to a profusion of images in its explication rather than to any consistent theory."[16] As was noted before, the term *Meshiach*, among others, was applied to Yeshua by his followers. Its meaning was inwardly transformed and gradually expanded. Eventually it came to be filled with the notion of divinity. That clearly was not the understanding of Yeshua himself nor of his first followers, as can be seen in the early layers of the synoptic gospels. Whether it was the understanding even in the later writings of the New Testament is now disputed. But, be that as it may, if what Yeshua thought, taught and wrought is taken as the ultimate measure of Christian doctrine, and he did not claim himself to be God, nor understand the term *Meshiach* to be infused with the notion of divinity when his contemporary followers were using it to refer to him, does that mean that Christians must abandon the traditional term "Christ"? Obviously not, as long as it is not given a meaning that stands in contradiction to how Yeshua would have understood it—*if it is to be identified with Yeshua exclusively.*

In fact, however, there are a number of contemporary Christian theologians who use the term "Christ" in a way which is *not* exclusively identified with Yeshua of Nazareth. John Cobb, for example, writes that "'Christ' is therefore a name for the Logos.... It refers to the Logos *as* incarnate."[17] Elsewhere he also rightly links up the *Logos* with the Hebrew *Hokmah/Sophia* (Wisdom) when he says, "I myself wish that the Johannine prologue had spoken of Sophia instead of Logos, and I propose that, despite the predominance of Word in the tradition, we speak today of Wisdom."[18] But he also makes the notion of Christ much broader than the manifestation of the *Logos* in Yeshua of Nazareth. Rather, Christ is "the process of creative transformation in and of the world.... All authentic thinking and speaking embodies this creative transformation as does all sensitivity of feeling and free imagination. Indeed life itself is the continuing expression of the Logos as creative transformation.... God or the Logos as incarnate is Christ."[19] In a way, the *Logos* is God *in se* and Christ is God *ad extra*, though the notions of incarnation and creative transformation also play central roles in Cobb's thought here.

He then goes on to speak of Yeshua being so one with the incarnate manifestation of the *Logos,* that is, with Christ, that Christ "coconstitutes with the personal past the very selfhood of" Yeshua.[20] He points out, however, that "there is no *a priori* basis for determining whether others have participated in this structure of existence. That remains an open question." But "so far as we know, Jesus is unique."[21] Cobb speaks similarly elsewhere when he writes that although "this Wisdom is incarnate in Jesus cannot mean that Jesus is the only channel through which God is present in the world...Jesus is the center of history for Christians."[22]

The key thing to notice here is that while on the one hand the Christian tradition is reaffirmed in that Yeshua is said to be a unique incarnation of the *Logos* and that he is consequently the center of history, on the other hand he is explicitly said not to be the only incarnation of the *Logos,* and is the center of history *for Christians.*

John Cobb is a Protestant theologian. This problem is also wrestled with by the Catholic theologian Raimundo Panikkar, who also speaks of Christ in a way not unlike Cobb's "creative transformation": "The thesis of the Unknown Christ is that... there is something in every human being that does not alienate Man but rather allows Man to reach fullness of being. Whether the way is transformation or some other process...this... principle exists. Christians have called it Christ, and rightly so."[23]

Clearly for Panikkar too the term Christ is understood very broadly, including all the manifestations of the divine. Problems arise with the exclusive identification of Christ with Yeshua of Nazareth, and to this issue Panikkar says that, "the Christ we are speaking of is by no means the monopoly of Christians, or *merely* Jesus of Nazareth."[24] He is so certain of this position that he writes: "That the historical name Christ should not be confined to the thus-named historical Jesus hardly needs mentioning here."[25] Panikkar, too, affirms that Yeshua is key for Christians, for it is through him that they come to God, but not only is the latter more important than Yeshua, so also is the world-pervasive manifestation of God, Christ. "It is in and through Jesus that Christians have come to believe in the reality that they call Christ, but this Christ is the decisive reality."[26]

In the thought of Panikkar obviously there is nothing of the exclusive identifying of Christ with Yeshua, as in the narrowly ontologically understood propositions that had become traditional in much of Christian thought. Christ for Panikkar (and Cobb) is a metaphor, a symbol—which gives the term not less but more importance; only a "materialistically" minded thinker would argue otherwise: "Christ has been and still is one of the most powerful symbols of humankind, though ambivalent and much-discussed."[27]

What does such an approach do to the Christian doctrine of the incarnation? John Hick addresses this question directly and argues that, whenever in Christian history "theologians have tried to spell out its meaning in literal, factual terms the result has been heretical.... And all attempts to treat the incarnation as a factual hypothesis have likewise been rejected by the church because they have failed to do justice either to Jesus' full humanity or to his full deity." He adds that "one may say that the fundamental heresy is precisely to treat the incarnation as a factual hypothesis! For the reason why it has never been possible to state a literal meaning for the idea of incarnation is simply that it has no literal meaning." Hick insists that the incarnation "is a mythological idea, a figure of speech, a piece of poetic imagery. It is a way of saying that Jesus is our living contact with the transcendent God.... Thus reality is being expressed mythologically when we say that Jesus is the Son of God, God incarnate, the Logos made flesh."[28]

This "new" way of understanding statements about Yeshua and Christ is in many ways reminiscent of the "old" way of understanding, namely, the "Jewish" way of Yeshua and his contemporaries discussed earlier. What are the chances that this metaphorical, symbolic way of understanding of these statements will be widely accepted outside of a coterie of theological experts? I am in substantial agreement with Hick when he says that the Christian mind will almost inevitably come to see the doctrines of the incarnation and the trinity in a new way, "no longer as precise metaphysical truths but as imaginative constructions giving expression—in the religious and philosophical language of the ancient world—to the Christian's devotion to Jesus as the one who has made the heavenly Father real to him." He notes that in physiological-psychological categories "this is the kind of development which the intellectual part of the Christian mind (appropriately, in the human brain, the left hemisphere!) is likely to undergo, while its more emotional other half perhaps continues to use the traditional language of Christian mythology without raising troublesome questions about its meaning."[29]

## 6. Conclusion

If, as we have argued, the purpose in gaining knowledge, truth, is to attain an ever fuller grasp of reality so we can live accordingly, and religion is the search for this knowledge at its deepest and most comprehensive level so we can shape our whole life accordingly, then I believe the answer to our question at the beginning of our reflections is clear. We asked whether it is possible for someone to come to wholeness, holiness, salvation by some path other than that of Yeshua the Christ. We looked at the need to understand the mythic, metaphorical use of language often employed in the Jewish Scriptures, both the so-called Old Testament and the New Testament, in order to understand those writings—and Paul's statement about "the world being reconciled to God through Christ" was used as a test case—and this led to a rejection of an exclusivistic understanding of salvation. We saw also how some prominent Catholic and Protestant contemporary theologians likewise understand the term Christ in a highly metaphorical way—in this following Paul's lead when he speaks of the "cosmic" Christ—and how this move frees the way of wholeness, salvation through Christ from being exclusivistically attached to the historical Yeshua.

But perhaps most conclusively, we saw that the present paradigm shift in our way of understanding truth statements away from an absolutist, monologic view of truth to a deabsolutized, perspectival, dialogic view not only means that we Christians can with integrity toward our own tradition hold that others can come to a life of wholeness, holiness, of salvation on paths other than that of Yeshua the Christ. It means also that we Christians, and all others, need dialogue with each other so that, in addition to attaining the grasp on reality that we can from our own perspectives and traditions, we may also come to an ever increasing understanding of reality by absorbing the insights others have into reality from their differing perspectives and traditions, which we are unable to attain from our own. Moreover, in this we Christians are following what Yeshua thought, taught and wrought, for concerning his followers he said: "I came that they may have life, and have it *ever more abundantly*" (Jn. 10:10).

## Notes

1. The careful word studies by Friedrich Büchsel in Kittel, *Theological Dictionary of the New Testament*, I, pp. 254 ff., and by other scholars in various reference works, really do not resolve the problem as we have posed it. It is clear from these studies that the word used by Paul (and he is only one who uses it in the New Testament), *katallassein*, and its variant *katallagenai*, fundamentally mean to change, and in this case to change the relationship between God and humanity in a positive direction, that is, to reconcile. *Theos en en Christo kosmon katallasson heauto* is how Paul put it in 2 Cor. 5:19, and Jerome translated it: *Deus erat in Christo mundum reconcilians sibi*. Of course the very notion of reconciliation in whatever language is perforce on the transphysical, "metaphorical" plane; it is not used to describe material, physical things, but rather the relationship between beings on the mental or psychological level. The word studies tend not to point out that obvious fact—perhaps because it is such an obvious given. But when the theologians go to work on the meaning of Paul's statements they often seem to be oblivious of this fact.

2. Cf. Joseph A. Fitzmyer, "Jesus the Lord," *Chicago Studies*, 17 (1978), p. 91.

3. David Tracy, *Blessed Rage for Order* (New York: Seabury Press, 1979), p. 108.

4. It is ironic that two Christian scholars, one a moderate Protestant and the other a moderate Catholic, should both use modern critical analysis—here mainly audience criticism (i.e., learning how the original audience would have understood words and phrases used so as to determine their meanings as intended by the New Testament authors)—to arrive at slightly differing conclusions, which when taken together document solidly that all the New Testament writers were using language metaphorically when speaking of Jesus in divinizing terms. The first, the Protestant James D. G. Dunn, argued that this was the case everywhere, except in some Johannine texts—specifically excluding the Pauline texts (*Christology in the Making* [Philadelphia: Westminster, 1980], pp. 210 ff.). The second, the Catholic Edward Schillebeeckx, argued

that this was the same everywhere, except in some Pauline texts—specifically excluding the Johannine texts (*Jesus* [New York: Seabury, 1979], pp. 556 ff.).

5. Hans Küng, *Christentum und Weltreligionen* (Munich: Piper Verlag, 1984), p. 187.

6. There are of course many issues that will need to be aired and resolved at this point; Christian scholars need to get on with this vital task. One of the objections likely to be raised by traditionalists is that this description of the meaning of Jesus Christ, i.e., Christology, is simply that of nineteenth-century liberal Protestantism. First of all, it is precisely the traditionalists who should know that merely pointing out that something has been said before does not thereby make it false. Moreover, given the huge advances in the scriptural sciences in the past hundred years, despite surface similarities, the differences between the two positions will also be significant. As to the problem of immutably fixing the interpretation of the scriptural gospel message in ontological language in the fourth and fifth centuries in Hellenistic Christianity, it should be remembered that—assuming that my argument, and that of many other scholars, is correct— the radical shift from metaphorical to metaphysical language was made once between the first and the fourth centuries, between the Semitic and Hellenistic milieux. *Ab esse ad posse*—if it happened, it's possible. Put otherwise: if it happened once, why not twice, or more times?

For example: A solemn decree from an ecumenical council can never be changed? Compare the following statements from two councils recognized to be fully ecumenical by the Roman Catholic Church: The sixteenth Ecumenical Council, Constance (1414-1418):

> This synod declares first that, being legitimately convoked in the Holy Spirit, forming a general council and representing the universal Church, it has immediate power from Christ, which every state and dignity, even if it be the papal dignity, must obey in what concerns faith, the eradication of the mentioned schism [there were three Popes at that time, the so-called Western Schism], and the reformation of the said Church in head and members. Likewise, it declares that whoever of whatever condition, state, dignity, even the papal one, refuses persistently to obey the mandate, statutes and orders of prescripts of this sacred synod and of any other general council legitimately convened, above set out, or what pertains to them as done or to be done, will be penalized and duly punished with recourse if necessary to other means of law.

Vatican Council I (1870) on the other hand stated:

> All the faithful of Christ are bound to believe that the holy apostolic See and the Roman pontiffs have the primacy over the whole world.... that the judgment of the apostolic See, whose authority has no superior, can be reviewed by none; and that no one is allowed to judge its judgments. Those, therefore, stray from the straight way of truth who affirm that it is lawful to appeal from the judgments of the Roman pontiffs to an ecumenical council—as to an authority superior to the Roman pontiff. (Quoted in Leonard Swidler, *Freedom In the Church* Dayton: Pflaum, 1969, pp. 92f.)

Again, if it happened once, it can happen again.

7. Hasan Askari, "Within and Beyond the Experience of Religious Diversity," in John Hick and Hasan Askari, eds., *The Experience of Religious Diversity* (Hants: Gower, 1985), p. 209.

8. Frances Young, "A Cloud of Witnesses," in John Hick, ed., *The Myth of God Incarnate* (Philadelphia: Westminster, 1977), p. 13.

9. Krister Stendhal, "Notes for Three Bible Studies," in Gerald Anderson and Thomas Stransky, eds., *Christ's Lordship and Religious Pluralism* (Maryknoll: Orbis, 1981), pp. 14f.

10. Paul Knitter, *By No Other Name?* (Maryknoll: Orbis, 1985), p. 261, has a helpful comment on the issue of the kind of language used and the understanding of its truth content:

> This is not to imply that there was no metaphysical truth in what the early Christians said or that they were conscious of this distinction between metaphysical and confessional language. If they could have made such a distinction, they most likely would have said that the cognitive or metaphysical content of their confessional language was that there was no one else like Jesus. I am suggesting that given the nature of their language, such metaphysical claims are not intrinsic to that language. Today, Christians can hear and use the same language with different metaphysical content.

11. Ibid., p. 183.

12. Cf. Schillebeeckx, *Jesus,* pp. 405 ff.

13. Cf. Rosemary Ruether, *To Change the World* (New York: Crossroad, 1981).

14. Ivan Havener, *Q The Sayings of Jesus* (Wilmington: Michael Glazier, 1987), p. 89.

15. John Cobb, *Christ in a Pluralistic Age* (Philadelphia: Westminster Press,1975), p. 132.

16. Ibid., p. 115.

17. Ibid., p. 76.

18. John Cobb, "Toward a Christocentric Catholic Theology," a lecture delivered at the conference "Toward a Universal Theology of Religion" held at Temple University, October 17-19, 1984. Published in Leonard Swidler, ed., *Toward a Universal Theology of Religion* (Maryknoll: Orbis Books, 1987), p. 88.

19. Cobb, *Christ in a Pluralistic Age,* p. 77.

20. Ibid., p. 142.

21. Ibid. John Hick expresses a similarly cautious view: "Whether he incarnated self-giving love more than anyone else who has ever lived, we cannot know. But we do know that his actual historical influence has been unique in its extent." *God Has Many Names* (Philadelphia: Westminster Press, 1982), p. 28. Judging from the description of the life and teaching of Yeshua and their subsequent influence, it would seem that Yeshua was uniquely "love-filled," "God-filled," in that sense. It is highly unlikely, though not certainly so, that such a life could have been lived elsewhere without having had similar effects. Moreover, even if we conclude from the lack of similar effects from other lives in the past, we cannot *a priori* exclude that possibility from the future. Metaphorically speaking, that would be to try to lock God in the box of human history, human past. See Dennis Nineham, "Epilogue," in Hick, *The Myth of God Incarnate,* pp. 186-204, where as a New Testament scholar he argues that the historical documentary evidence available is inadequate to claim moral perfection for Yeshua.

Most recently E. P. Sanders summed up this view:

> We cannot say that a single one of the things known about Jesus is unique.... The combination can doubtless be called 'unique', but that shows that he was an individual and not a two-dimensional representative of a type.... We cannot even say that Jesus was a uniquely good and great man.... History, in fact, has grave difficulty with the category 'unique'.... It is, rather a fault of New Testament scholarship that so many do not see that the use of such words as 'unique' and 'unprecedented' shows that they have shifted their perspective from that of critical history

and exegesis to that of faith. We can accept without argument Jesus' greatness as a man, but we must stop well short of explaining his impact by appeal to absolutely unique personal qualities. What is unquestionably unique about Jesus is the result of his life and work. (E. P. Sanders, *Jesus and Judaism* [Philadelphia: Fortress, 1985], pp. 319 ff.).

22. Cobb, "Christocentric Theology."
23. Raimundo Panikkar, *Unknown Christ*, p. 29.
24. Ibid., p. 49.
25. Ibid., p. 27.
26. Ibid., p. 29.
27. Ibid., pp. 26f.
28. Hick, *God Has Many Names*, pp. 74f.
29. Ibid., pp. 125 ff.